DISABILITY, CULTURE, AND EQUITY SERIES

Alfredo J. Artiles, *Series Editor*

INTERSECTIONALITY IN EDUCATION

TOWARD MORE EQUITABLE POLICY, RESEARCH, AND PRACTICE

EDITED BY

Wendy Cavendish
Jennifer F. Samson

Foreword by Sonia Nieto

TEACHERS COLLEGE PRESS

TEACHERS COLLEGE | COLUMBIA UNIVERSITY
NEW YORK AND LONDON

Published by Teachers College Press,® 1234 Amsterdam Avenue, New York, NY 10027

Copyright © 2021 by Teachers College, Columbia University

Front cover illustration by David Connor

Library of Congress Cataloging-in-Publication Data

Names: Cavendish, Wendy, editor. | Samson, Jennifer F., editor.
Title: Intersectionality in education : toward more equitable policy, research, and
    practice / edited by Wendy Cavendish, Jennifer F. Samson ; foreword by Sonia
    Nieto.
Description: New York, NY : Teachers College Press, [2021] | Series: Disability,
    culture, and equity series | Includes bibliographical references and index.
Identifiers: LCCN 2020054595 (print) | LCCN 2020054596 (ebook) |
    ISBN 9780807765128 (paperback) | ISBN 9780807765135 (hardcover) |
    ISBN 9780807779453 (ebook)
Subjects: LCSH: Educational equalization—United States. | Intersectionality
    (Sociology)—United States.
Classification: LCC LC213.2 .I58 2021 (print) | LCC LC213.2 (ebook) | DDC
    379.2/6—dc23
LC record available at https://lccn.loc.gov/2020054595
LC ebook record available at https://lccn.loc.gov/2020054596
ISBN 978-0-8077-6512-8 (paper)
ISBN 978-0-8077-6513-5 (hardcover)
ISBN 978-0-8077-7945-3 (ebook)

Printed on acid-free paper
Manufactured in the United States of America

Contents

PART III: APPLICATION OF
INTERSECTIONALITY-BASED ANALYSIS IN RESEARCH

Foreword

As a new middle school teacher some 50 years ago, I was focused on improving the lives of the students I taught, all of whom were Puerto Rican or African American. Having grown up in similar circumstances as many of them, I thought I understood what their lives were like. I soon learned that I had only a partial lens for understanding them. Yes, like me, they were children of color, most lived in poverty, and the parents of many were immigrants with a limited formal education who spoke little or no English. There were also many differences that defined us. I came from a tight-knit nuclear family with lots of extended family nearby, while some had no network of support. In my family, we spoke Spanish at home, while some of my students spoke only English and some spoke other languages. My brother had autism, although that term was not in use at the time; nor did we hear the words "special education" until many years later. Although all of us were seen as "minorities," the terminology used at the time, we differed in phenotype, race, and ethnicity. My students' families had arrived in New York City either from Puerto Rico (as mine had), from other Caribbean nations, or as part of the Great Migration of African Americans from U.S. Southern states. My family had arrived in the early part of the 20th century when jobs, even for those with a limited education, were plentiful. There were also differences in our immigrant status, gender, and gender identification, among other differences of which I was completely unaware at the time. These included involvement in the criminal justice system, homelessness, and being raised in foster care. Looking back, I realize now that knowing about these differences would have given me a deeper understanding of my students and, in the process, would no doubt have made me a better teacher.

The term *intersectionality*, and indeed the study of multiple and intersecting identities and realities, has become widespread in a number of fields, including very prominently in education. In fact, intersectionality as a theoretical framework is now widely recognized as a central way to gain a better grasp of the totality of any number of issues, identities, and institutions. In this book, editors Wendy Cavendish and Jennifer Samson and their chapter authors include in their analyses such disparate areas as law, criminal justice, school and out-of-school policies and practices, interrupted schooling, and the kinds of research that are considered in each of these.

By linking these matters, the editors insist that self-reflection and viewing others through multiple intersections can help educators gain a deeper and more complete picture of any given issue in order to move towards meaningful action. The title itself—*Intersectionality in Education: Toward More Equitable Policy, Research and Practice*—underscores the need to understand the deep connections between intersectionality and equity.

Many of us in education have dedicated our professional lives to studying and advocating for equity and justice in education. Yet we've often done so by focusing on only one, or a small number, of aspects of equity. This is partly due to the tremendously complicated issues involved, as well as to the partial knowledge and experiences educators and researchers have about many of the issues. Partly it is also due to a fear of "diluting" our main concern, whether that be race, social class, language, or any other identity. This was certainly the case years ago when incorporating LGBTQ issues under the umbrella of multicultural education was controversial, though I'm glad to say that it is much less true today.

The nine chapters in this book will have your head reeling with insights that you may never have considered but that, once you have, help you understand how very logical they are when viewed through an intersectional paradigm. Here, there is something for everyone interested in delving more deeply into what it means to use intersectionality as a lens to understand individuals as well as systems. What is particularly significant is how the authors consider all of these issues in a comprehensive yet unapologetic way. For example, the intersectionality-based analysis (IBA) guiding questions (see Table I.1) are an excellent example of how intersectionality works across disciplines, policies, and practices. Every educator and every researcher should read, consult, and learn from these questions. Thought-provoking and probing, they are certain to raise the level not only of readers' awareness, but perhaps also of their discomfort in recognizing their own blind spots and shortcomings.

Both theoretical and practical, the authors' many recommendations for policy, practice, and action will challenge readers to rethink about how to understand inequity in education and what to do about it. They may also be challenged in how they see the world. But this is, after all, how we best learn: by considering multiple perspectives, by challenging our own sacrosanct ideas, and by changing our minds and actions. To quote the ever-inspiring and always relevant John Dewey:

> Conflict is the gadfly of thought. It stirs us to observation and memory. It instigates invention. It shocks us out of sheep-like passivity, and sets us at noting and contriving . . . conflict is a *sine qua non* of reflection and ingenuity. (Dewey, 1922, p. 300)

It is my hope, then, that as you read this book—whether you are a teacher, professor, researcher, or policymaker—you will have a bit of your worldview disrupted. Not only will you benefit, but so will our students, our schools, our universities, and, ultimately, our society.

—Sonia Nieto

REFERENCE

Dewey, J. (1922). Morals are human. In *Human nature and conduct: An introduction to social psychology* (pp. 295–302). Modern Library.

Introduction to Intersectionality-Based Analysis

Jennifer F. Samson and Wendy Cavendish

The collaborative journey embarked on to develop this book began in 2015, born from a convening of scholars, researchers, policymakers, teachers, parents, and students around the topic "Intersections of Race and Class in Special Education Policy." The colloquium examined and challenged the systemic inequities within the field of special education that result in disproportionate placement of certain subgroups based on race, gender, and/or language status in special education. We recognized the need for clarification on how to engage in intersectional analyses of oppressive legislative practices that are particularly harmful to individuals who are subject to marginalization due to identity labels of being Black, non-English speaking, poor, disabled, or all of the above.

In light of the devastating year that was 2020, unlike at any point in recent history, intersectional issues have taken center stage at a national scale against the backdrop of a global pandemic due to COVID-19, economic uncertainty, and widespread racial and social unrest. Given the prevailing demographic backgrounds of current leaders and policymakers—typically wealthy, White, and male—we question how decades of "equity-focused" policies have largely failed to live up to their promises to address systematic oppression based on race, gender, disability, sexual orientation, culture, class, language, or citizenship status. Those with the privilege and power to write policies, allocate resources, and enact practices to benefit "others" from disadvantaged demographic categories are rarely asked to reflect on their own identities. They are never asked to be transparent about who they are and how their bias-tinged worldviews affect the decisions they make, problems they identify, and solutions they propose. They rarely tolerate the inconvenience of having to answer to the populations for whom policies are being written to see if the problems and solutions being proposed make sense.

Thus, efforts to address persistent inequality in education reflect a long history of education reform policies and practices that have largely failed to achieve the promise of equal protection under the law for children and youth of all backgrounds. Biases and discrimination on the

1

basis of race, class, disability, and language status have resulted in local, state, and federal mandates that data be disaggregated based on these categories. However, the reports that are generated rarely take into account the impact on students who are subject to further marginalization when they are assigned more than one of these identity variables. It can lead to unacknowledged differential and accumulated effects that are not accounted for in many educational policies. Intersectionality is a theoretical framework proposed by Kimberlé Crenshaw (1991) that accounts for the complex, overlapping, and cumulative effects associated with having more than one identity marker that can lead to systematic exclusion or added marginalization within institutions and structures even when they claim to be advancing equity. Crenshaw's early work was based on case studies of Black women who were systematically and legally denied employment due to race and gender bias. In this book, we build upon Crenshaw's intersectionality theory and also adapt Olena Hankivsky and colleagues' (2014) intersectionality-based policy analysis framework that is composed of key questions that were developed specifically to address health disparities but have applicability within the interconnected systems that affect educational outcomes. Hankivsky's framework acknowledges multiple dynamic identities that change over time, insists on critical self-reflection, and is intentionally equity focused. Notions of power and privilege are central to the use of intersectionality as an analytic lens and distinct from work that simply includes two or more identity markers (Collins, 2015). Thus, this intersectionality-based framework can be used as a specific analytic tool for understanding and examining the complexity of social conditions and experiences in education to potentially identify steps in practice, policy implementation, and research that move beyond considerations of "fairness" to identifying specific, actionable steps for increasing equity.

For this volume, the framework was adapted for the purposes of addressing disparities in educational policy, research, and practice and includes intersectionality-based analysis (IBA) guiding questions. Our interdisciplinary authors consider IBA at multiple levels (i.e., local, district, state, federal, societal) and across disciplines (i.e., education, law, policy, criminology, juvenile justice, foster care, and indigenous studies).

The chapters assembled in this volume provide case examples of how equity-focused IBA approaches show promise for undoing imperfect systems that fail to take into account how individuals are more complex than a singular category. At the heart of every system are individuals, and the IBA approach begins with critical self-reflective questions where stakeholders are asked questions about their own individual identities that often carry unique biases about how to frame problems and solutions. Other IBA questions encourage decisionmakers to be sure to engage key stakeholders who are closest to the issues. The full complement of IBA guiding questions for equity-focused policy and research analysis are provided in Table I.1.

Table I.1. Intersectionality-Based Analysis (IBA) Guiding Questions for Education Policy and Research (Adapted from Hankivsky et al., 2014)

Policy & Practice	Research
Who are you and what motivates you to do this work?	
Who is being studied and why?	
What knowledge, values, and experiences do you bring to this area of policy or practice?	
What social determinants (race, gender, class, citizenship, etc.) affect your perspective?	
How have representations of the "problem" come about? How has the framing of the "problem" changed over time or across different spaces?	Who is the research for? Does it advance the perspectives of those under study?
How are groups differentially affected (privileged/oppressed) by this representation of the "problem"?	Is the research framed within context? Does it reflect self-identified needs of affected groups/communities?
How do existing policies and practices address, maintain, or create inequities between different groups?	Is the sample representative of the experiences of diverse groups of people for whom the issue under study is relevant?
Which are the important intersecting social locations and systems? For example, how do race, ethnicity, class, ability, and systems of inequality (racism, colonialism, classism, ableism) interact in relation to this problem?	Is the tool of inquiry suited to collecting micro or macro data, or a combination of both?
Where and how can interventions be made to improve the problem? What are the available policy levers?	How are interactions at individual levels of experience linked to social institutions and processes of power?
How will proposed responses reduce inequities?	What issues of domination/exploitation and resistance/agency are addressed by the research?
Who will be responsible (and who is best positioned) to ensure the implementation of the recommendations?	How will commonalities and differences be recognized without resorting to essentialism, false universalism, or obliviousness to historical patterns of inequality?
How will implementation and outcomes be measured?	
How will affected communities/diverse representatives be meaningfully engaged in assessing the reduction of inequities?	

What you will find in this book are nine chapters written by authors whose scholarly work considers the differential impact of structural and institutional inequity associated with being designated as one or more of the following: poor, Black, Indigenous, disabled, homeless, English language learner, immigrant, foster care-involved, or juvenile justice-involved. There is increasing consensus that in order to be truly equity focused, one must be intersectionality based, and here we invite you as the reader to consider what this means in practice. We pose that there is utility in intentionally adapting an IBA approach to better understand and address educational disparities. The collection of chapters in this book provide compelling examples of equity-focused intersectionality approaches that include critical self-reflection as well as critical inquiry into how inequity is framed and addressed in order to undo and disrupt the prevailing structures systems of oppression throughout society.

ORGANIZATION OF THE BOOK

Part I is focused on cross-disciplinary theoretical considerations of intersectionality from the perspective of social systems, educational law and criminology. This is followed by Part II and the application of the IBA framework to understand federal legislation and district policies that address the needs of foster care and homeless youth, as well as immigrant English language learners. Part III includes chapters that apply the IBA frame to education research at the community and individual level.

Chapter 1, by Leigh Patel, starts Part I by considering how policies are delivery systems for "justice" that lead to harm and death for Black and Brown bodies in society at large as well as within schools. Chapter 2 by Osamudia James describes how landmark High Court cases in education resulted in formal legal commitments to equality that have had the paradoxical effect of undermining universal equality due to neglecting intersectionality. In Chapter 3, Amie Nielsen points out how overlapping themes in education and criminology can be beneficial to understanding complex and problematic issues in both fields such as "zero tolerance" and the "school-to-prison pipeline" through the application of racial threat, labeling, and social disorganization theories.

In Part II, authors provide examples of IBA in policy applications, beginning in Chapter 4 with Kele Stewart and Wendy Cavendish's consideration of child welfare and special education policies as part of a longitudinal study on a transition program for foster youth. Next, in Chapter 5, Deborah Perez unpacks federal legislation associated with homelessness for youth and the need for more nuanced attention to how it can better serve constituents in need of essential services. In Chapter 6, Kristen Kibler considers policy supports within a study of teachers of immigrant English language learners who enter school late and who have had interrupted schooling in their countries of origin.

Part III begins with Chapter 7, a study by Patrice Fenton, who examines the experiences of Black male special education teachers' identity within schools using a critical race theory lens. Chapter 8, by Wendy Cavendish, centers youth perspectives in considering how the juvenile justice system could employ intersectional approaches to supporting youth who face challenges with reentry. Finally, in Chapter 9, Aydin Bal, Aaron Bird Bear, Dosun Ko, and Linda Orie describe the collaborative development of the Indigenous Learning Lab, an exemplar of sociohistorical and intersectional consideration within the building of a community-focused research project. In the Conclusion, we editors return to summarize the utility of IBA as demonstrated across the chapters, with the goal of establishing a way to address educational disparities so as to make progress in achieving educational equity for all.

We invite all readers to engage with the chapter authors' application of intersectionality-based policy and research analysis as models of equity work from which to draw for self-reflection and activist stance development. We hope that the work provided by these scholars may inspire readers' own contributions to dismantling patriarchy, colonialism, racism, sexism, ableism, xenophobia, and homophobia.

REFERENCES

Collins, P. H. (2015). Intersectionality's definitional dilemmas. *Annual Review of Sociology, 41*, 1–20.

Crenshaw, K. (1991). Mapping the margins: Intersectionality, identity politics, and violence against women of color. *Stanford Law Review, 43*(6), 1241–1299.

Hankivsky, O., Grace, D., Hunting, G., Giesbrecht, M., Fridkin, A., Rudrum, S., Ferlatte, O., & Clark, N. (2014). An intersectionality-based policy analysis framework: critical reflections on a methodology for advancing equity. *International journal for equity in health, 13*(1), 119.

Part I

INTERSECTION OF SYSTEMS AND DISCIPLINES

CHAPTER 1

Delivery Systems and Intersectional Vulnerability

Leigh Patel

In pharmacology and the medical field at large, delivery systems are generally understood to be the ways in which various drugs are administered and then affect the bio- and neurophysical systems. For example, a pill that has an external coating would have a time-released delivery to its intended system (e.g., circulatory, nervous, gastrointestinal), while one without such a coating would act immediately. As I write this chapter, I am practicing physical distancing, as the pandemic of COVID-19 has drastically upended life for millions around the planet and has led to loss of life and intensified vulnerability. The pandemic has its own delivery system of transfer among living beings. The reaction to the pandemic is both backdrop and example for this chapter, as it reflects many of the points that I address in how delivery systems might provide us a more precise lens of analysis of the ways intersectional vulnerability is heightened through certain population-level delivery systems. In this chapter, I aver that how we ascertain intersectional vulnerabilities and harms can be enhanced more precisely through the metaphor and reality of differential delivery systems.

INTERSECTIONALITY

A now-common term in academic and many activist arenas, intersectionality had a long history before a term was attached to it. When Sojourner Truth asked in a 1851 speech, "Ain't I a woman," she was shining a light on the intersections of racism and patriarchy as defined through slavery and its afterlife. The Combahee River Collective wrote their statement in 1983. It was the product of years of study of the sources and impact of violence toward Black lesbians in Boston, but its name is an homage to the rebellion led by Harriet Tubman in 1863. In her now-classic theorization of the insufficiencies of single-node social categories, Crenshaw (1991) introduced intersectional analysis to legal studies of discrimination. She drew attention to the matrix of oppression Black women experienced that could not be adequately ascertained through a focus solely on either race or gender. Using single-node analyses rendered Black women's experiences untellable, as the legal and societal analysis either silenced gender through anti-racist lenses or race through feminist lenses. Intersectionality offered a lens of analysis that showed how processes of racialization coalesced with patriarchy, economic stratification, and heteronormativity to result in wholly different vectors of subjugated experiences of society. Crenshaw argued that these specific coordinates of subjugation were unrecognizable by the law, because of its insistence on a uniform experience through either race or gender and its linear argument that demanded one social location of oppression to take precedence and therefore invalidate the other social location. Crenshaw, who situates her work in the tradition of Black women theorists including Anna Julia Cooper, postulated that while intersectional analyses may seem intuitive to many, "It's not as though the existing frameworks that we have—from our culture, our politics or our law—automatically lead people to being conversant and literate in intersectionality" (as quoted by Adewunmi, 2014, para 6). It is an ongoing challenge to contend with intersectional oppression because, as demonstrated through essentialized understandings of culture, the broader context is permeated by more static definitions of social categories (Roberts, 2009).

The existing frameworks that Crenshaw referred to have particular resonance in the legal field, which is predicated upon categories of people. As legal scholar Cheryl Harris carefully documented in her now classic article, "Whiteness as Property" (1993), legal designations of whiteness and its concomitant rights, including the baseline expectation of those rights, formed the foundation of legal precedents and laws that protected property as a form of whiteness. Crenshaw's work complements Harris's analysis by illuminating the ways that intersectional social locations, such as being dis/abled and Black, are not merely an additive function, but create differential social locations of vulnerability.

For example, when Eric Garner, a Black man who had worked for the city's horticultural department but quit due to health stressors, was choked to death in 2014 by New York City Police Department officer Daniel Pantaleo, his last 11 sentences were repetitions of "I can't breathe!" A medical examiner, after an autopsy, concluded that Garner died from a fatal level of asthma (a documentable disability), caused by a cascade of lethal effects that were precipitated by the officer's unrelenting chokehold on Garner (Winston, 2019). Pantaleo was fired from his post as an NYPD officer and has since filed a civil lawsuit for wrongful dismissal.

Garner's life and death offer an apt example for thinking about interlocking delivery systems of harm and vulnerability. After his death, many people on social media posted disparaging remarks about Garner's size. These comments reflect the all too common reality of meritocracy (Guinier,

2015), the widely held fallacy that one's station or social location in society is completely due to one's own will, ethic of hard work, and innate talent. In Garner's case, meritocracy acted as a delivery system of both judgment and backward justification of his murder, ascribing the fault to him and his apparent lack of self-control. Fat-shaming is just one way that meritocracy delivers narrative rewards for those who do not live this reality and narrative punishment for those who do. Social media comments also indicted Garner in his own death because he had heart disease, a condition that was responsible for 23% of all U.S. deaths in 2015, according to the Centers for Disease Control (https://www.cdc.gov/heartdisease/facts.htm). In Garner's case the delivery system of vulnerability from heart disease was connected to environmental racism, yet he was subject to posthumous narrative punishment and individualized blame for his own death.

Eric Garner also lived with asthma, a condition that is overrepresented in poor neighborhoods whose residents are mostly Black or brown (Maantay, 2007). Communities of color deprived of high standards for air quality have disproportionate levels of asthma in both children and adults. As the coronavirus has spread rapidly around the planet in 2020, asthma has not been personalized as an individual flaw, nor as a population-level vulnerability for many poor and working class, racially minoritized peoples. Asthma, it seems, when it includes people of means across race, class, gender, and ability categories, is no longer a delivery system of meritocracy. Rather, it is simply a risk factor. And yet the statistics of deaths from COVID-19 reveal the undeniable existing susceptibility to already marginalized peoples. Naively first referred to as an equal opportunity virus, due to its high level of contagion, the virus has revealed the enduring fact that being poor and Black creates vulnerabilities into which the virus hooked into.

Notably, while schools, workplaces, and myriad places to gather were shut down, police and vigilante violence did not pause during the pandemic. Within the space of a few weeks in the summer of 2020, at least seven Black people were murdered by police or extralegal vigilantes. In a horrific and all too common echo of Eric Garner's murder, George Floyd, a Black man in Minneapolis, was similarly killed through the literal extinguishing of his breath. White police officer Derek Chauvin knelt with his full body weight on George Floyd's neck for 8 minutes and 45 seconds while four other police officers looked on. This murder, in addition to others (including Breonna Taylor, who was shot seven times in her home because police had a "no-knock entry" policy), sparked the global uprisings that have led to public pedagogies of protests demanding that the police be defunded so that the first responders to people in need of various forms of help will not be a white supremacy–fueled militarized police force. The protests have not only raised awareness. As in all social movements, they educate the public about injustice through the direct action of marches, sit-ins, and walkouts.

POPULATION-LEVEL DELIVERY SYSTEMS

In her renowned book *Golden Gulag*, Ruth Wilson Gilmore defined racism as the "population-level suffering and acceleration to death" (2007). This definition is reflected in Garner's murder, and far too many others, in which Black, Indigenous, and other peoples of color are deemed to be expendable or cageable for profit. These patterns of acceleration to harm and death through legal and extralegal violence point to the systems of delivery through which harm is exacerbated by policies that intertwine across local, state, and federal systems, disproportionately and purposefully creating harm for Black, Indigenous, and queer people, and people of color. For example, in a 2015 article in the *Washington Post*, Emily Badger reported on "million dollar blocks," single city blocks in poor and deprived neighborhoods. The phrase, which Badger adopts from social geographer Laura Krugan and Justice Project analyst Eric Cadora, describes the pattern in which so many people from single city blocks are detained and/or incarcerated that the costs to taxpayers, and the profits for private and public detainment and incarceration facilities, clock in at millions of dollars. In this example, the delivery system of harm is obviously also connected to the delivery system of wealth and wellness for a few. These systems include delineated local policing policies, state judicial codes, and federal policy investments in impunity for a carceral state. In fact, this is one of the key aspects of delivery systems: the duality of suffering of many and wellness and wealth for a few, codified through de jure and de facto practices.

All too often, delivery systems of harm are coded through institutional processes that perpetuate white supremacy and, in essence, gaslight people of color for the harm they experience in a world that weaponizes societally incurred health challenges as a way to blame people for their own deaths. In the cases of both Garner and Floyd, their homicides were tied in the autopsy reports to conditions of, respectively, asthma and coronary disease. As noted by a group of physicians (Crawford-Roberts et al., 2020), both of George Floyd's autopsies (a second autopsy was demanded after the first was challenged for its inadequacies) linked his death to the condition of his heart. As the physicians detailed, this left people who had watched the horrific video of breath being literally squeezed out of this man to reconcile how a medical condition that impacts over years could be put into play for a homicide that occurred in 8 minutes and 45 seconds. This kind of coding, seemingly professional and therefore beyond reproach by people who have not attended medical schools, is a keen example of the insidious, long-standing, deeply engineered machinery of white supremacy that weaponizes anyone deemed not to have a disability. This codification of autopsy report is one of the niche areas in which policing of bodies, death, and disability converge to systematically incentivize and remove consequences to legal and extralegal murders. This pattern of impunity routinely spins the dial of blame toward entire populations.

Delivery systems are also acting when they fail to provide for the material, spiritual, and intellectual needs of a community. The above examples speak to subjugated populations in urban areas, but rural communities bear a different kind of outcome from paucity of resources and even the non-existence of delivery systems for life-sustaining materials. In 2019, seven hospitals in rural Georgia closed, leaving the majority of the state's geography without even remote access to healthcare. Compounding that paucity of delivery systems for wellness, the coronavirus pandemic has exacerbated and brought into sharp contrast that even the facilities that remain open are sorely underequipped to contend with the illnesses that many poor, rural, and, in the case of Georgia, Black people experience—hypertension, heart disease, diabetes, and more—socioeconomically shaped conditions of co-morbidity (Ebell et al., 2017). At the time of this writing, more than a quarter of Georgia's deaths due to COVID-19 have occurred in one rural county, Dougherty (Millet et al., 2020).

UNSETTLING MODERNITY AND COLONIALITY

My use of delivery systems is not to classify them wholesale as good or bad. Much like technological tools, the rub is in what is delivered through these systems, what is not, and how knowing that can help us to see and analyze more precisely how population harm happens, all too commonly, through intersections of power and oppression. When the editors of this volume convened the equity-focused policy colloquium, our agenda, conversations, and duty were to address how disability must reckon with various other forms of oppression. It is important to note that as a person who has a documented disability, I do not consider myself as disabled but as a human being whose boundaries have been more clearly defined by my neuro- and bio-physiology. Moreover, those boundaries have not been shaped solely through my genetic code but are in active dynamic with my contexts and daily life demands. Put more simply, a categorical designation cannot contend with myriad dynamically interacting factors that temporarily shape access, ability, and wellness.

One of the resounding themes of the gathering of these authors was a veritable piercing through disciplines set asunder through the culture of the academy. In fact, having panels composed of legal scholars, decolonial scholars, and special education experts allowed for, and in fact demanded, a cross-cutting dialogue about the lived realities of multiply minoritized populations. The gathering was powerful; this volume conveys much of that power as well as providing impetus for praxes for equity that cannot manifest through singular disciplinary research projects.

In a recent exchange with a colleague who is steeped in Afrofeminist literature, we discussed a game, or exercise, that poses a number of crucial questions when considering what must be changed, scrapped, and/or imagined for delivery systems to provide wellness for all. For me, at this moment, and during our convening in 2016, the question that stays, rankles, and makes me commit again and again to collective praxes for equity is: What do we need to let go of in order to lift up possibilities?

There is no doubt in my mind that the categorization and disciplinary isolation of special education, critical race theory, gender studies, and coloniality has to date institutionally weakened the potential for transformative social change. Fittingly, while I write during the COVID-19 pandemic and global uprising against anti-Black racism, the imperatives of connectivity, and collective, and freedom dreaming have risen to the fore in the minds of community organizers, healers, and cultural workers. The question of what we are willing to give up to reckon with how deeply we are connected has been forced upon us all at the crux of a pandemic and a global rebellion. Although it's been there all along, a global pandemic puts into neon light the reality that we have already had to give things up (deadlines for deadlines' sake, squabbling over student stipends when their vulnerability has risen to the top of priority conversations). What more fundamentally must we give up to truly contend with the intersectional vulnerability so many people with dis/abilities live with?

I refuse the fallacy that vulnerabilities are a reflection of biological determinism, lack of merit, or even bad luck. By refusing this fallacy, I invite a reckoning with the reality that overdetermining vulnerability within marginalized populations is an affront to humanity itself. As an educator, I must also contend with the fact that formal schooling has acted as one of the most efficient delivery systems for intersectional harm since the arrival of European settlers on Turtle Island.

To act from this stance, I and other educators are answerable (Patel, 2016) to several recommendations, including the fact that inclusion cannot exist without transformation. As Martin Luther King Jr. confided to his friend and fellow activist Harry Belafonte, "I fear that I have been fighting for our people to gain entry into a burning house." Inclusion has been a mainstay of special education, and its disruption of practices that exclude anyone outside of a Euro-descendant and patriarchal definition of *normal* has been crucial to the field. However, the inclusion of people within fundamentally racist, ableist, and heteropatriarchal systems driven by the production of test scores and disability labels is tantamount to acquiescing to the harm that awaits them. To adequately contend with this recommendation to think about social transformation rather than inclusion, we'd do well to remember that no social movement is ever about a single issue, such as the right to vote or the right to equitable education, but rather about social transformation at its core. These movements, including the Black Lives Matter movement, have been about the irreducible demand that living beings are not to be used for profit, ownership, or spectacle of suffering. There is no single discipline that can tackle that demand, but working across disciplines opens up opportunities by giving up silos.

REFERENCES

Adewunmi, B. (2014, April 2). Kimberlé Crenshaw on intersectionality: "I wanted to come up with an everyday metaphor that anyone could use." *New Statesman.* https://www.newstatesman.com/lifestyle/2014/04/kimberl-crenshaw-intersection-ality-i-wanted-come-everyday-metaphor-anyone-could

Badger, E. (2015, July 30). How mass incarceration creates 'million dollar blocks' in poor neighborhoods. *Washington Post.* https://www.washingtonpost.com/news/wonk/wp/2015/07/30/how-mass-incarceration-creates-million-dollar-blocks-in-poor-neighborhoods/

Combahee River Collective. (1983). The Combahee River Collective statement. In B. Smith (Ed.), *Home girls: A Black feminist anthology* (pp. 264–74). Women of Color Press.

Crawford-Roberts, A., Shadravan, S., & Tsai, J. (2020). George Floyd's autopsy and the structural gaslighting of America. *Scientific American.* https://blogs.scientificamerican.com/voices/george-floyds-autopsy-and-the-structural-gaslighting-of-america/

Crenshaw, K. (1991). Mapping the margins: Intersectionality, identity politics, and violence against women of color. *Stanford Law Review, 43*(6), 1241–1299.

Ebell, M., Marchello, C., & O'Connor, J. (2017). The burden and social determinants of asthma for adults in the state of Georgia. *Journal of the Georgia Public Health Association*, 6(4), 426–434. https://doi.org/10.21633/jgpha.6.406

Gilmore, R. W. (2007). *Golden gulag: Prisons, surplus, crisis, and opposition in globalizing California.* University of California Press.

Guinier, L (2015). *The tyranny of the meritocracy: Democratizing higher education in America.* Beacon Press.

Harris, C. I. (1993). Whiteness as property. *Harvard Law Review*, 106(8), 1707–1791.

Maantay, J. (2007). Asthma and air pollution in the Bronx: Methodological and data considerations in using GIS for environmental justice and health research. *Health & Place, 13*(1), 32–56.

Millett, G. A., Jones, A. T., Benkeser, D., Baral, S., Mercer, L., Beyrer, C., Honermann, B., Lankiewicz, E., Mena, L., Crowley, J. S., Sherwood, J., & Sullivan, P. S. (2020). Assessing differential impacts of COVID-19 on black communities. *Annals of Epidemiology, 47*, 37–44. https://doi.org/10.1016/j.annepidem.2020.05.003

Patel, L. (2016). *Decolonizing educational research: From ownership to answerability.* Routledge.

Roberts, D. E. (2009). Race, gender, and genetic technologies: A new reproductive dystopia? *Signs: Journal of Women in Culture and Society, 34*(4), 783–804.

Winston, A. (2019, May 15). Medical examiner testifies Eric Garner dies of asthma caused by officer's chokehold. *New York Times.* https://www.nytimes.com/2019/05/15/nyregion/eric-garner-death-daniel-pantaleo-chokehold.html

CHAPTER 2

Law, Identity, and Access to Education

Osamudia James

Landmark legal cases that address the issue of equality often implicate education. From *Brown v. Board's* prohibitions on schooling segregation in 1954, to *Grutter* and *Gratz's* guidelines regarding college and university affirmative action in 2003, to *Parents Involved's* declarations regarding race-conscious K–12 assignment policies in 2007, the cases that contour equal protection in the United States simultaneously shape education policy in both K–12 and higher education.

Trends in equality law, therefore, can deeply impact education, with a potentially attenuated focus on identity in ways that undermine commitments to equal educational opportunity. In particular, a commitment in American law to formal, but not substantive, equality preserves and aggravates education disparities based on differences in identity. Formal equality ultimately subjects race-conscious remedies to heightened judicial scrutiny that curtails or outright prohibits needed solutions to racial inequality.

Universal equality frameworks undermine targeted identitarian interventions designed to address disparities. Although consideration of the needs of humans absent identity markers has utopian appeal, universal frames like dignity neither disrupt nor interrogate implicit norms about which identities inform the universal subject. Between a presumption of illegitimacy regarding the use of identity, whether benign or invidious, and a reluctance to tailor interventions for populations in need of them, policymakers and legal actors undermine education policies that would have the capacity to improve educational outcomes.

Advancing education equity in the United States, therefore, will necessarily require cross-disciplinary focus that considers the intersection of education and law. Such a focus not only more fully illuminates the dynamics of power and marginalization, but also locates the intersecting social and political systems that must be engaged if substantive educational equality is to be finally achieved.

FORMAL, BUT NOT SUBSTANTIVE, EQUALITY

In the United States, claims of discrimination in violation of equal protection are subject to a complicated system of review. Courts extend tiered levels of scrutiny that provide more or less rigorous interrogation of governmental classifications based on identity. Black racial identity, in particular, was an initially protected class. Later, the U.S. Supreme Court extended legal solicitude to other identity groups that have been targets for exclusion and discrimination, including groups that have been "saddled with disabilities or subjected to . . . a history of purposeful unequal treatment, or relegated to . . . a position of political powerlessness as to command extraordinary protection from the majoritarian political process"; "been subject[] to discrimination"; or "exhibit obvious, immutable, or distinguishing characteristics that defend them as . . . discrete groups."[1] These extensions came to encompass additional racial and ethnic groups (Knouse, 2009), women, and children of nonmarital parentage, while excluding gays and lesbians, the poor,[2] and the disabled. To the extent that our equal protection is anchored in identity groupings, the cornerstone of equal protection jurisprudence is identitarian in nature.

Despite the Supreme Court's laudable attempt to recognize how identity shapes equality, equal protection has nevertheless been undermined by the Court's accompanying commitment to formal rather than substantive equality. Pursuant to formal equality modes, both benign and invidious racial classifications are subject to the same forms of judicial scrutiny. Based on this reading of equal protection, the Supreme Court has preserved facially neutral laws with disparate impact on minority groups as long as discriminatory intent cannot be found, while also prohibiting race-conscious government policies with the capacity to ameliorate racial inequality.

Using this approach to equality, the Supreme Court has eroded protections against racial discrimination in labor and employment (holding that societal discrimination was insufficiently compelling as a justification for a minority business enterprises set-aside program),[3] criminal justice (upholding the Georgia death penalty despite conclusive evidence showing that even after taking account of nonracial variables, defendants charged with killing White victims were 4.3 times as likely to receive a death sentence as defendants charged with killing Black victims)[4] and other spheres of American life. As noted legal scholar Ian Haney López has remarked, when assessing inequality through a formal lens, we get racism and racial remediation exactly backward (Haney López, 2006).

Nor has educational policy been immune to this inversion. During the early aughts, Seattle, WA, adopted a controlled-choice school assignment policy meant to account for racial segregation in the area schools. The Seattle school district was segregated by White and non-White peoples, with Whites enjoying near-exclusive access to the city's better schools on the north side of the city (Liu, 2008). Attempting to break the monopoly of White parents on access to these schools, the school assignment policy primarily considered parent preference when making school assignment policies, but considered race whenever the racial demographics of particular schools began to skew toward White or non-White racial isolation.[5] A group of White parents, frustrated by the use of race as a potential obstacle to receiving their preferred schools assignment, eventually challenged the policy on equal protection grounds.

In *Parents Involved v. Seattle School District No. 1*, the Ninth Circuit affirmed the assignment plan, with a judge noting, in particular, that the controlled-choice plan had none of the problems of typical race-conscious affirmative action programs: The plan was adopted to promote public school integration rather than segregation; the plan was neither meant to suppress minorities nor did it have that effect; there was no attempt to give a particular group additional political power based on skin color; no race was given preference over another; and although denial of preferred school assignment might have been disappointing, it bore no relationship to an individual student's aptitude or ability.[6]

Seattle's controlled-choice program is an example of the benign use of race in the school system. Rather than using race to maintain racial isolation or give parents particular advantages, the school district instead paid attention to race in service of integration and equal opportunity. Although race-conscious policies can always be abused, the Seattle school district protected the integrity of the policy by considering White and non-White isolation, avoiding hazy notions of merit in assignment decisions, and using race only as a tie-breaker once a school became oversubscribed.

The Supreme Court, however, ultimately struck down the controlled-choice plan as unconstitutional. In a concurring opinion meant to carve out spaces in which race-conscious school assignment plans might be permissible, Justice Kennedy cautioned against the harms of defining students by race,[7] warning that "reduc[ing] [an] individual to an assigned racial identity for differential treatment is among the most pernicious actions" government can take."[8]

The Court's assessment of race-conscious controlled-choice policies is an example of how equal protection jurisprudence in the United States prioritizes formal equality over substantive equality. The Court adopts a presumption of illegitimacy regarding the use of racial classifications, no matter the methods or end goals. According to the Court's analysis, racial classification, it seems, is as pernicious, if not more so, than the disparate outcomes that stem from a segregated schooling system, or the monopoly White parents in Seattle enjoyed over the city's most successful schools. As such, facially neutral educational policies, like school assignments by residence or assignment lottery parameters, that are most easily navigated by powerful parents pass constitutional muster because they do not formally implicate race. At the same time, educational policies adopted to maximize integration and mediate disparities are prohibited because they take specific account of race.

This inversion in equality continues to animate attacks on race-conscious policies adopted to facilitate equality, particularly in higher education. Despite a 2003 decision permitting the use of race as one factor among many to consider in university admissions,[9] affirmative action is again on trial. In suits against Harvard University and the University of North Carolina at Chapel Hill, plaintiffs again allege the impermissible use of race. Key aspects of litigation strategy are novel; the suit against Harvard University, for example, alleges that Asian Americans are disadvantaged in an admissions scheme that gives other minority groups undue advantage (Hartocollis, 2018). Nevertheless, the presumption regarding the use of race as illegitimate anchors the suits, and is aided by a jurisprudence more concerned with formal reference to race than actual racial disparities.

UNIVERSALITY AS A MEANS OF CREATING EQUITY

At the same time that the Court's commitment to mere formal equality endures, a second concerning trend in the law threatens to perpetuate education inequality: The embrace of *universality* in equality law. Universal approaches to equality encourage movement away from identity groups as the relevant unit of interrogation and comparison in antidiscrimination regimes. Instead, all individuals, without reference to their identity, are guaranteed a set of rights, benefits, or protections. A universalist approach to civil rights, then, is one that either guarantees a uniform floor of rights or benefits for all persons or, at least, guarantees a set of rights or benefits to a broad group of people not defined according to the identity axes highlighted by our antidiscrimination laws (Bagenstos, 2014). In the employment context, a universalist approach to workplace protections is part of a "larger trend of expanding civil rights protections beyond rules that prohibit discrimination to rules of universal applicability" (Clarke, 2011, pp. 1221–1222).

Vulnerability theory, for example, is anchored in recognition of a shared and inevitable human vulnerability, and capitalizes on an acknowledgment that disadvantage, even independent of racial and gender biases, can operate as an galvanizing political tool (Fineman, 2008). Under the vulnerability framework, institutional arrangements are the targets of protest and political mobilization, thus eliminating the need to organize interest groups around identity (Fineman, 2008).

The concept of dignity similarly moves away from identity, and is common in human rights discourse. The language of dignity has been central in both the United Nations Charter and the Universal Declaration of Human Rights (McCrudden, 2008). In the United States, the concept of dignity featured prominently in *Obergefell v. Hodges*,[10] the Supreme Court's land-mark decision striking down state bans on same-sex marriage.

Supreme Court jurisprudence further reflects fatigue regarding identitarian equality claims. In the Court's 2007 *Parents Involved* opinion concerning K–12 integration, Roberts made the Court's impatience with race and remedy quite explicit, striking down race-conscious integration plans while asserting that "the way to stop discriminating on the basis of race is to stop discriminating on the basis of race."[11] Unsurprisingly, then, the Court has been moving away from group-based equality claims under the guarantees of the Fifth and Fourteenth Amendments to "dignity claims" rooted in the due process guarantees of the same (Yoshino, 2011, p. 748).

There is debate about what constitutes a universal equality movement. Labor movements, for example, are not grounded in race, gender, or ethnicity, although they are still plausibly grounded in the identity category of poor or working class. The presidential campaigns of 2016 and 2020 featured uncertainty about such movements; the economic redistribution policies on which presidential candidate Bernie Sanders campaigned sparked debate about what sorts of movements—race or economics—would successfully improve long-term outcomes for Blacks in the United States (Johnson, 2016; Spence, 2016).

Despite debate, the appeal of universal equality frames is obvious. Most fundamentally, universality can address the deficiencies of equal protection. The Court, for example, has limited equal protection primarily to race and ethnicity, religion, and gender, meaning that categories like class or sexual orientation are not covered. Indeed, in 1973, the Supreme Court rebuffed a challenge to school finance laws that allocated funding on the basis of property taxes, thus nullifying any argument that discrimination on the basis of class might constitute an equal protection violation of the U.S. Constitution.[12] Universality, therefore, would make broader claims based not on poverty versus wealth, but rather anchored in adequacy of resources for all students. Universality purports to build coalitions, and can stave off the "pluralism anxiety" (Yoshino, 2011, p. 748) that sometimes informs equality backlash.

In conjunction with a commitment to formal equality, however, universality in the law can perpetuate, rather than ameliorate, inequality. Universality does not, for example, disrupt implicit norms about who is the universal, and thus "ideal," subject. In its focus on all citizens, appeals to universal equality can mask an implicit understanding of Whites as the ideal baseline, and non-Whites as problematically deviated from that baseline. Moreover, as long as policies embedding these norms do not formally reference race, they will fly under constitutional radar.

Consider, for example, the development of the 2001 No Child Left Behind Act. The harmful focus on standardization and high-stakes testing that marks the legislation is informed by a deficit orientation toward the non-White students at whom the legislation was aimed. Not embodying the universal ideal, children affected by the racial achievement gap that school reform initiatives like NCLB are meant to target are subject to harsh and punitive policies (Lawrence, 2006). Moreover, the disparate impacts of these policies are generally legitimate under a formal equality regime, even as they produce substantive inequalities. Calls to move away from identity without making the implicit normalization of White racial identity, and accompanying denigration of non-White identity, less opaque will only leave white supremacy undisturbed.

Further, universal policies, although potentially less vulnerable to legal and social challenge, nevertheless miss opportunities for targeted interventions that ameliorate racial inequality, particularly given the failure of race-neutral policies like those based on income to improve outcomes (Jones & Nichols, 2020). Ultimately, all parents want quality education for the children in their care. However, if White, middle-class, able-bodied, and heterosexual people are implicitly embedded in our notion of the universal subject, then parents, caregivers, and families that deviate from that unstated norm will have needs that go unaddressed in our bid for universality. While the demand of White parents to end excessive high-stakes testing can benefit all students, working-class parents or families of color may also seek an end to racialized disciplinary and academic tracking practices at their schools—an important school reform goal that may be lost in the priority that universal policy frames give to White parents. Similarly, White, middle-class families are better situated to take advantage of the school-choice trend in education reform, using material, social, and cultural capital more easily in school choice markets. In contrast, families of color are more likely to find that their choices are constrained in the education market by resources, race (James, 2014), and even intentional exclusion (Butler, 2015). A commitment to improvements that are purportedly good for everyone risks camouflaging how race dictates whose desires are prioritized and characterized as good for everyone.

CONCLUSION

What is ultimately needed is more than noting merely whether the language of education policy is neutral, or asking whether policy prescriptions are good for "everyone." Rather, educational equality requires interrogating the disparities that even race-neutral policies can produce, and leveling intentional and specific focus on the needs of students who are typically marginalized in American schools. This focus interrogates not only when existing policy does not contemplate minority students, but also when it *does* by embedding notions of inherent deficit.

Pushing back, then, on commitment to language rather than substance, and to universal rather than targeted interventions, is integral to advancing equality writ large, and education policy more specifically. Both lawyers and educators must continue to demand an interpretation of equal protection that is substantive rather than formal, and that builds on antisubordination models that permit the active remediation of discrimination, even in the absence of intentional discrimination. Moreover, universalist approaches to equality, like human rights or dignity, should be cautiously deployed. Although not without value, they have the potential to mask the tendency of policy to favor the already advantaged. Finally, even when targeted interventions are adopted, implicit assumptions about the communities served, and how those assumptions dictate implementation and participation, must be interrogated.

NOTES

1. San Antonio Indep. Sch. Dist. v. Rodriguez, 411 U.S. 1, 28 (1973); Bowen v. Gilliard, 483 U.S. 587, 602-03 (1987). Korematsu v. United States, 323 U.S. 214 (1944).
2. San Antonio v. Rodriguez, 411 U.S. 1 (1973).
3. City of Richmond v. Croson, 488 U.S. 469 (1989).
4. McClesky v. Kemp, 481 U.S. 279 (1987)
5. Parents Involved in Community Schools v. Seattle School District No. 1, 426 F.3d 1162 (9th Cir. 2005).
6. Parents Involved in Community Schools v. Seattle School District No. 1, 426 F.3d 1162, 1194 (9th Cir. 2005) (Kozinski, concurring)
7. Parents Involved in Community Schools v. Seattle School District No. 1, 127 S.Ct. 2739 (2007).
8. Parents Involved in Community Schools v. Seattle School District No. 1, 127 S.Ct. 2739 (2007).
9. Grutter v. Bollinger, 539 U.S. 306 (2003).
10. Obergefell v. Hodges, 576 U.S. 644 (2005).
11. Parents Involved in Cmty. Sch. v. Seattle Sch. Dist. No. 1, 127 S. Ct. 2738, 2768 (2007).
12. San Antonio Indep. Sch. Dist. v. Rodriguez, 411 U.S. 1, 28 (1973).

REFERENCES

Bagenstos, S. (2014). Universalism and civil rights (with notes on voting rights after *Shelby*). *The Yale Law Journal, 123*, 2838–2876.
Butler, A. (2015, January 16). South Miami, UM building 'racial disparity' case against Somerset. *Miami Herald*. https://www.miamiherald.com/article7057199.html
Clarke, J. (2011). Beyond equality? Against the universal turn in workplace protections. *Indiana Law Journal, 86*, 1219–1289.
Fineman, M. A. (2008). The vulnerable subject: Anchoring equality in the human condition. *Yale Journal of Law & Feminism, 20*, 1–25.

Haney López, I. F. (2006, November 3). Colorblind to the reality of race in America. *The Chronicle of Higher Education.* https://www.chronicle.com /article/colorblind-to-the-reality-of-race-in-america/

Hartocollis, A. (2018, October 13). What's at stake in the Harvard lawsuit? Decades of debate over race in admissions. *The New York Times.* https://www.nytimes .com/2018/10/13/us/harvard-affirmative-action-asian-students.html

James, O. (2014). School choice as racial subordination. *Iowa Law Review, 99,* 1083–1135.

Johnson, C. (2016, February 3). An open letter to Ta-Nehisi Coates and the liberals who love him. *Jacobin.* https://www.jacobinmag.com/2016/02/ta-nehisi-coates -case-for-reparations-bernie-sanders-racism/

Jones, T., & Nichols, A. H. (2020, January 15). Hard truths: Why only race-conscious policies can fix racism in higher education. *The Education Trust.* https://edtrust.org/resource/hard-truths/

Knouse, J. (2009). From identity politics to ideology politics. *Utah Law Review, 749,* 120–142.

Lawrence, C. (2006). Who is the child left behind?: The racial meaning of the new school reform. *Suffolk University Law Review, 39,* 699–718.

Liu, G. (2008). Seattle and Louisville. *California Law Review, 95,* 277.

McCrudden, C. (2008). Human dignity and judicial interpretation of human rights. *The European Journal of International Law, 19,* 655–675.

Spence, L. K. (2016, February 2). Reparations and the racial residual. *Baltimore City Paper.* https://www.baltimoresun.com/citypaper/bcp-020316-reparations-lester -spence-20160202-story.html

Yoshino, K. (2011). The new equal protection. *Harvard Law Review, 124,* 748–49.

CHAPTER 3

Overlapping Interests

Contributions of Criminology for Schools and Education Policy

Amie L. Nielsen

While education and criminology often remain in separate spheres, the two disciplines have many overlapping interests as well as much to offer each other. For example, various educational outcomes (e.g., disproportionate punishment for racially and ethnically marginalized students) are of interest to criminologists, school failure is a leading risk factor for delinquency, and "zero-tolerance" policies and the "school-to-prison pipeline" entail fundamental mechanisms and processes relevant to both disciplines.

In this chapter I seek to highlight some of the ways that criminology can benefit education by addressing the role of sociological mechanisms impacting delinquent behavior, school processes, and some educational outcomes (Hirschfield, 2018). I discuss three theoretical perspectives and issues in criminology that are salient for reviewing and critiquing education policy, especially related to punishment. I highlight some of the ways that these criminological theories (racial threat, labeling theory, and social disorganization) may provide frames to critically analyze and assess education discipline policies (especially zero tolerance) and the educational processes and outcomes linked with delinquency and police contact.

I approach this chapter from multiple standpoints. I am a professor at the University of Miami, and I have training in, teach, and conduct research in criminology. I am also a White, middle-class woman, so I attend to the issues contained within from a place of privilege. I am further privileged in other ways. I attended high school between 1984 and 1988, a period that preceded some of the punitive policies addressed here. While I was suspended once during high school, rather than being ostracized and subject to labeling processes described in this chapter, I was welcomed back and reintegrated. Like most adolescents (Moffitt, 1993), I engaged in some forms of delinquency and crime. Fortunately, I escaped my youth without an official delinquent or criminal record because I was not caught for my misbehaviors. My life today would likely be very different had things been otherwise. I am aware that my privileged place in the world as a White female helped shield me from the more damaging implications of youthful wrongdoings, and that many others are not so lucky.

CRIMINOLOGY

Criminology is a discipline often closely connected with sociology. Many criminologists focus on social and structural factors that influence individual behavior and/or the behaviors of organizations and institutions in society. Criminologists have long identified school factors as associated with involvement in delinquency and crime, and increasingly schools are dealing with aspects of the juvenile and criminal justice systems. Concerns about school violence have resulted in a whole host of policy and procedural changes, including "zero-tolerance" policies related to misbehavior and discipline, and the increasing presence of armed school resource officers and armed teachers (Hirschfield, 2018; Kupchik, 2016).

This chapter's emphasis is on matters specific to criminology and education, including how and why criminological theory can inform adolescent delinquency and the implications of school responses to student misbehavior and delinquency. I focus on the work of sociologists and criminologists to highlight some of the possible insights these disciplines may offer to education. I do not address every criminological theory with potential relevance here. Instead, I highlight three that provide theoretical frames with which to examine education policy, schools, and delinquency. Specifically, I focus on racial threat theory (Blalock, 1967; Blumer, 1958), labeling theory (Lemert, 1951), and social disorganization theory (Shaw & McKay, 1969). Other criminological theories, such as strain theories (e.g., Agnew, 2006), social control/bond (Hirschi, 1969), and the general theory of crime (Gottfredson & Hirschi, 1990), also speak to relationships involving schools, education, and delinquency (e.g., Gottfredson, 2001; Hirschfield, 2018) and may be of interest to readers.

To address these issues, I first give an overview of key education policies related to school discipline and the school-to-prison pipeline. I next address racial threat theory to address disparities in use and application of such disciplinary policies as well as their implications. I then utilize labeling theory to help expand upon and seek to explain how school punishment is implicated in creating the pipeline. I then highlight another theory, social disorganization, to discuss delinquency, school violence, and education resources and quality. Throughout, I am guided by the intersectionality-based analysis (IBA) frame presented by Samson and Cavendish in the Introduction to this volume (adapted from Hankivsky et al., 2014), and I particularly seek to address the following questions: (1) How do existing policies and practices address, maintain, or create inequities between different groups? (2) How are groups differentially affected (privileged/oppressed) by this representation of the problem? and (3) Which are the important intersecting social locations and systems? Much of this discussion is focused on racial and ethnic disparities.

SCHOOL DISCIPLINE AND THE SCHOOL-TO-PRISON PIPELINE

Criminologists are paying increasing attention to the school-to-prison pipeline. This term refers to processes in which disciplinary responses that occur at school or related to school (e.g., on the bus) may result in immediate or eventual entanglement in the juvenile justice or criminal justice systems. It is in part a byproduct of major changes in educational policies. Specifically, changes in the 1990s and after were prompted by concerns related to high-profile school shootings (e.g., the 1998 Jonesboro and 1999 Columbine killings) and school violence (Cavanagh et al., 2019; Hirschfield, 2018; Kupchik, 2016). Changes in security and other policies were intended to make schools and students safer physically, psychologically, and emotionally, and to provide for a better learning environment by removing potentially violent youth (Cavanagh et al., 2019; Kirk & Sampson, 2011).

These educational policy changes are part of the broader context of "getting tough" on juvenile delinquency and crime that started in the 1980s (see, e.g., Garland, 2001; Kupchik, 2016; Simon, 2009). These educational changes were supported by federal policies (e.g., 1994 Safe and Drug-Free Schools), grants (e.g., Secure Our Schools and COPS in Schools), and incentives. Such changes include increased reliance upon zero-tolerance policies and the use of new security measures (e.g., metal detectors, drug-sniffing dogs), as well as many schools hiring School Resource Officers (SROs). Zero-tolerance policies call for automatic suspension and expulsion for certain behaviors. SROs are police officers stationed at schools, providing on-site security in the event of dangerous situations (Hirschfield, 2008; Kupchik & Ward, 2013; Payne & Welch, 2010; Welch & Payne, 2012).

While intended to improve school safety and student well-being, these changes have many negative implications. For example, punitive and zero-tolerance policies disempower youth and teach them that they have limited rights. This undermines the school climate by reducing perceptions of fairness, caring, and trust (Hirschfield & Celinska, 2011; Kupchik, 2009). Schools focus attention on punishment and rules rather than on education of youth (Bowditch, 1993; Kupchik, 2009; Na & Gottfredson, 2013). Students who are suspended lose learning time and have lower reading and math achievement scores than other youths. This is particularly evident for

Black and Latinx youths relative to Whites, students in special education, and students in lower socioeconomic groups. Moreover, in schools with above-average suspensions, non-suspended students' achievement is negatively impacted, particularly in schools in which violence levels are lower (Perry & Morris, 2014). Zero-tolerance policies arguably impact youths' educational opportunities and aspirations in ways that violate their civil rights. In many communities those hit hardest are racially and ethnically marginalized youth and their families, as alternative educational options may not be available in the local communities or families may lack the resources to afford them (Cavanagh et al., 2019).

Large percentages of students are suspended and/or expelled every year. Data for 2015–2016 show that across K–12 schools about 2.7 million students were suspended and almost 121,000 expelled (U.S. Department of Education, Office for Civil Rights, 2019). While the presence of SROs does provide on-site security, SROs also deal with behavioral problems and can arrest students suspected of delinquency or crime (Kupchik & Ward, 2013; Na & Gottfredson, 2013; Payne & Welch, 2010; Wolf & Kupchik, 2017). In-school arrests are often for minor forms of misbehaviors, resulting in the criminalization of what formerly were typically considered common adolescent behaviors (Hirschfield, 2008; Na & Gottfredson, 2013; Simon, 2009). In 2015–2016, over 290,000 students were arrested at school or referred to law enforcement (U.S. Department of Education, Office for Civil Rights, 2019). Students arrested for incidents unrelated to school that occur off campus may be suspended or expelled (Hirschfield, 2008; Kirk & Sampson, 2013).

These educational policies and connections with the justice system are directly relevant to questions raised in the IBA framework (adapted from Hankivsky et al. [2014] by Samson and Cavendish; see p. 3, Table I.1, this volume). Concerning the first question, "How do existing policies and practices address, maintain, or create inequities between different groups?," these policies clearly do maintain and create inequities. They do so by producing differential access to education, negatively affecting the educational experience for all students, and reducing educational achievement especially for suspended youths but for schools overall, as well as increasing the likelihood that students will have contact with the juvenile or criminal justice system. All have long-term implications for life chances, as discussed below. Related to question two, "How are groups differentially affected (privileged/oppressed) by this representation of the problem?," all students and young people are impacted by these policies. However, racially and ethnically marginalized students, poorer students, and students in special education are particularly affected negatively. For question three, "Which are the important intersecting social locations and systems?," both educational policies and the criminal justice system are implicated, along with government (local, state, and federal), given funding and grant policies and the "get tough on crime" approaches that have permeated all levels of government.

DISPARITIES IN EXCLUSIONARY DISCIPLINE

As noted above, about 2.7 million students in K–12 were suspended at least once in 2015–2016, representing 5–6% of all students, and about 121,000 were expelled. Over 290,000 students were arrested at school or were referred to law enforcement (U.S. Department of Education, 2019). Use of these exclusionary forms of punishment in schools is not equally distributed. Minoritized youths and poorer youth are particularly likely to be referred to the school administration (Morris & Perry, 2017), suspended, or expelled from school (Jacobsen, Pace, & Ramirez, 2019; Morris & Perry, 2016; Owens & McLanahan, 2020; Skiba et al., 2011), even after accounting for school and area crime (Hughes et al., 2017). Students in special education are also at increased risk. Students arrested at school or referred to law enforcement are disproportionately Black, predominately male, and disproportionately students with disabilities (U.S. Department of Education, 2019). As such, these policies help to maintain and exacerbate inequities among students, an issue directly relevant to the first IBA question considered here.

Taking into account student behavior does not account for racial and ethnic disparities in exclusionary discipline. That is, with one exception (Wright et al., 2014), studies that control for student misbehavior (e.g., Jacobsen et al., 2019; Owens & McLanahan, 2020; Peguero & Shekarkhar, 2011; Rocque & Paternoster, 2011) show that racially and ethnically disparate rates of suspension or expulsion remain. Accounting for offense types, Whites were less likely than Black and Latinx students to receive expulsion or out-of-school suspension. Blacks and Latinx were more likely than Whites to be expelled or suspended for specific offenses, particularly less serious offenses that tend to be judged more arbitrarily (Skiba et al., 2011; see also Nicholson-Crotty et al., 2009). As Kupchik (2016) notes, such racial and ethnic disparities in school punishment serve to extend inequalities that currently exist and help to perpetuate them in the future.

Ethnic and particularly racial differences appear to be due to greater likelihoods of being referred to the office by teachers (Morris & Perry, 2017; Skiba et al., 2002). However, the "offense" leading to the referral may be more subjective (e.g., disrespect, excessive noise, disobedience) for Black students than for Whites (left class without permission, smoking) (Morris & Perry, 2017; Skiba et al., 2002). Others also note that female students of color may be especially likely to be punished via office referral for being "unladylike" and for violations of "normative femininity" standards (Kupchik, 2016; Morris, 2005; Morris & Perry, 2017). As such, students of color may be subject to higher levels of scrutiny and therefore subject to identification of violations because some teachers view them as threatening, oppositional, or dangerous (Morris, 2005).

RACIAL THREAT THEORY

Policy changes and practices of zero tolerance are not evenly implemented across schools (Hirschfield, 2008; Hirschfield & Celinska, 2011; Owens, 2017; Payne & Welch, 2010). For example, punitive zero-tolerance policies are more likely to be used in schools with higher poverty levels (proportion of students qualifying for reduced/free lunch over 50%) (Kupchik & Ward, 2013; Owens & McLanahan, 2020; Payne & Welch, 2010; Welch & Payne, 2010). Such findings hold even after accounting for other important factors such as in-school deviant behavior and poverty rates (Welch & Payne, 2010). Use of exclusionary school discipline and reliance on zero-tolerance policies also vary based on the racial and ethnic compositions of schools (Kupchik, 2009; Kupchik & Ward, 2013; Owens & McLanahan, 2020; Welch & Payne, 2010).

Racial threat theory offers important insights into why these disparities may exist. Racial threat theory grew out of the work of Blumer (1958) and Blalock (1967). The fundamental premise is that when Whites begin to view non-Whites (often African Americans but Latinx as well) as threatening their economic and/or political hegemony, they react in ways that seek to stem that threat. Racial and ethnic threat are often assessed by scholars in terms of the relative size or proportion of the non-White population, with threat felt more intensely by Whites as the size of the non-White population grows. When the size of the non-White population begins to grow, Whites tend to support punitive policies, including more police, greater use of incarceration, and use of the death penalty (Jacobs & Carmichael, 2001, 2002; Keen & Jacobs, 2009; Kent & Jacobs, 2005).

Racial threat has implications for schools and education. In terms of how this approach connects with schools, Rocque and Paternoster (2011) argue that "cultural threat" may be more important than economic or political threat. Specifically, they state:

> School discipline can be understood within the context of racial threat theory because teachers (especially white teachers), with their culture of academic success and need for control over the school environment, may easily perceive black students as a source of trouble or a threat to their ability to control the cultural context of what goes on within the school. (p. 639)

As the size of the Black student population grows, at least up to a certain point, it may be viewed as threatening the teachers' dominance, and punitive methods are used to increase social control (Rocque & Paternoster, 2011).

Research supports the racial threat approach in the area of education. Higher percentages of Black student populations are associated with higher rates of suspension and disciplinary practices (e.g., Hughes et al., 2017;

Jacobsen et al., 2019; Owens & McLanahan, 2020; Payne & Welch, 2015; Rocque & Paternoster, 2011) and less use of restorative practices, such as mediation and community service (Payne & Welch, 2015; Welch & Payne, 2010). In addition, the greater the percentage of Latinx students, the more likely that harsher punishments are employed (Hughes et al., 2017; Payne & Welch, 2010). At the county level, higher levels of racial disproportionality in school suspensions are strongly predictive of racial disproportionality in juvenile court referrals (Nicholson-Crotty et al., 2009).

As one example of application of racial threat theory, Rocque and Paternoster (2011) used a racial threat framework to examine whether elementary school students in schools in one state were referred to the vice principal's office for misconduct and how many times this occurred. Using multilevel models, they showed that net of individual-level misbehaviors, closeness with the teacher, personality (introversion), and other factors, as well as teacher and school effects, Black youths were more likely than White or Hispanic youths to be referred and to be referred more often. Referrals were more likely as the percentage of the school comprised of Black students increased.

Payne and Welch (2010) examined use of punishment in a sample of 294 public secondary schools. Net of numerous school controls (e.g., student delinquency, concentrated disadvantage), the percentage of students who were Black was related to the likelihood that schools used extreme punitive measures (e.g., court action, calling the police), zero-tolerance policies (automatic suspension), and punitive responses (suspension, in-school suspension, detention). The percentage of students who are Black was negatively related to the use of mild disciplinary and restitutive disciplinary policies.

Hughes and colleagues (2017) examined racial and ethnic threat for suspensions in a sample of Florida schools. Accounting for school- and district-level controls, they found support for this approach. Schools with larger percentages of Black students in the student body have a larger proportion of Black student out-of-school suspensions than of White student suspensions. Similarly, in schools with larger percentages of Latinx students, the proportion of Latinx students suspended was higher than for White students. Overall, in contrast to other studies showing that schools with greater percentages of racially and ethnically marginalized students are punitive to all, their results show that Black and Latinx students are the ones who "bear the brunt of any resulting punishment" (p. 604). They also showed that schools whose board members were more racially and ethnically diverse had few racial and ethnic disparities in suspensions.

Security measures utilized tend to differ across schools based on their racial and ethnic compositions. Specifically, schools with higher concentrations of racially and ethnically marginalized students are particularly likely to utilize metal detectors, and those with larger percentages of students who receive free lunch were especially likely to use metal detectors, police officers, and drug-sniffing dogs, although school-level (elementary, middle, secondary) variations were found (Kupchik & Ward, 2013). Kupchik and Ward (2013) state that

> the specific exclusionary security measure of metal detectors is more common in schools serving large numbers of youth of color. . . . This result suggests that racial/ethnic minority youth are exposed at greater rates to a practice that seeks to identify offending youth and divert them to the criminal justice system. With regard to poverty . . . exclusionary security policies are more common among elementary and middle schools but not high schools. Thus, poverty seems to mark younger children as potential threats requiring exclusionary control measures (p. 348).

LABELING THEORY

The use of exclusionary discipline such as suspension and expulsion, along with arrests by SROs, has critical implications for students. Labeling theory offers important insights into how suspension, expulsion, and arrest may lead to involvement in the school-to-prison pipeline.

Labeling theory has a long history in criminology. Originally articulated by Lemert (1951) and others, and drawing from its roots in symbolic interactionism (Snipes et al., 2019), the theory argues that as a result of "primary deviance," the initial deviant action, other people label that person as deviant. Importantly, one does not actually have to have engaged in the act; the consequential issue is that others believe that one has done so. Through a variety of processes, being labeled as "deviant" has very negative implications (Bernburg et al., 2006).

Labeling and resulting processes can occur through informal means, such as by friends. However, when labeling occurs through formal means, including by teachers, police, and the juvenile justice system, the implications are more severe (Matsueda, 1992). Use of zero-tolerance and exclusionary policies in schools, even after accounting for rates of disciplinary problems, increases students' likelihood of contact with juvenile and criminal justice systems and thus their likelihood of being labeled as deviant or criminal (e.g., Kupchik & Ward, 2013; Welch & Payne, 2010, 2012). Notably, adding SROs in schools over time has been related to more drugs and weapons offenses recorded and to greater numbers of less serious violent incidents (e.g., fighting without weapons) reported to police, thereby leading to formal labeling of youths for some behaviors that in the past would likely not have resulted in contact with the system (Na & Gottfredson, 2013; Owens, 2017).

The processes through which labeling is thought to lead to negative outcomes are multiple. For example, youth labeled as delinquent may reduce their prosocial connections to other people and gravitate toward youths similarly labeled (Bernburg et al., 2006; Wiley et al., 2013). Negative effects of labeling may include youth disengagement and alienation, disrupted student learning, greater surveillance of labeled youths, and other factors (Wolf & Kupchik, 2017). Wiley and colleagues (2013) used labeling theory to examine implications of police contact for youths. They show that youths who are arrested subsequently experience lower grades and lower school commitment compared to those who have no police contact. Both lower grades and lower school commitment are directly associated with a greater likelihood of engaging in delinquency. Lower grades help to account for a small (but significant) proportion of the effects of arrest on subsequent delinquency. Similarly, youths who are stopped by police but not arrested compared to those without contact have reduced grades and school commitment, although for this group only lower grades are associated with subsequent delinquency, both directly and indirectly (through police contact).

Despite what is known about labeling processes thus far, numerous scholars call for more attention to be paid to the ways schools and teachers impact the labeling processes for youths who have been in trouble at school and/or arrested (Bernburg & Krohn, 2003; Kirk & Sampson, 2013; Mowen et al., 2019; Rocque & Paternoster, 2011; Wiley et al., 2013). Regardless of the specific mechanisms, there are a multitude of negative outcomes associated with suspension, expulsion, and/or arrest, and they are often attributed to labeling processes linked with schools. Being suspended or expelled is associated with greater involvement in offending, with each additional suspension increasing crime and delinquency even with prior offending taken into account (Mowen et al., 2019). Regardless of actual delinquency, suspended youths are more likely to be arrested subsequently (Mowen & Brent, 2016). Long-term implications for adult incarceration are linked to suspension also (Wolf & Kupchik, 2017).

Arrests as well as involvement in the juvenile justice system are associated with higher likelihoods of dropping out of school (e.g., Hirschfield, 2009; Sweeten et al., 2009). Kirk and Sampson (2013) report that all youths in their study who spent time in a juvenile facility eventually dropped out. In addition, students who are arrested are less likely than non-arrested youth to go to college (Kirk & Sampson, 2013). Moreover, youths who are arrested and/or labeled as "troublemakers" by teachers are more likely to drop out of high school (Bernburg & Krohn, 2003; Kirk & Sampson, 2011, 2013) or be pushed out of school by schools themselves (Bowditch, 1993).

Lower levels of educational attainment, including having less than a high school degree, have important and severe implications in adulthood.

These implications include lower prospects for employment and economic well-being, and greater likelihood of adult arrest for males, especially Black males (Bernburg & Krohn, 2003; Pettit & Western, 2004; Western, 2002). As such, both the educational system and the juvenile justice system are implicated in creating and maintaining disparities among students and also have implications for adult well-being.

Thus, justice system contact impacts educational outcomes, which directly and indirectly influence delinquent and criminal behavior. Teachers/schools play other roles in labeling students and potentially leading to their involvement in juvenile/criminal justice systems (Cavanagh et al., 2019; Duran, 2013; Rios, 2011; Rocque & Paternoster, 2011). Racially and ethnically marginalized youths often believe that (largely White) teachers think they are the ones who start trouble and that they have lower academic expectations for students, undermining their ability to succeed (Padilla, 1993; Rosenbloom & Way, 2004). Stereotyping through labeling leads to frustration, poorer academic performance, and potentially to dropping out (Katz, 1997; Padilla, 1993; Rodriguez, 2005).

SOCIAL DISORGANIZATION THEORY

As discussed above, exclusionary educational policies are more likely to be used in schools with higher poverty levels and larger proportions of racially and ethnically minoritized students (Kupchik, 2009; Kupchik & Ward, 2013; Owens & McLanahan, 2020; Payne & Welch, 2010; Welch & Payne, 2010). Such schools typically are located in impoverished, "disorganized" areas. Thus, social disorganization theory has implications for educational policies and school outcomes.

Social disorganization theory deals with neighborhood factors and processes relevant for delinquency and crime rates. As originally articulated by Shaw and McKay (1969), communities have varying levels of social disorganization. Key structural characteristics of disorganized neighborhoods are economic disadvantage (including poverty, male joblessness, and other factors), residential instability (people move in and out of the community at high rates and there are high levels of property vacancy and low levels of home ownership), and racial and ethnic heterogeneity. These characteristics impede communication and undermine social control (Snipes et al., 2019). More recent work on social disorganization theory highlights mechanisms such as collective efficacy (social cohesion, shared expectations, and informal social controls), density of personal networks, and connections to local government, which are important for social control efforts and thus controlling crime in neighborhoods (e.g., Sampson, 2012; Sampson et al., 1997; see Sampson et al., 2002).

Systemic factors contributing to disorganized and impoverished neighborhoods have numerous implications for schools and education. Students who live in impoverished neighborhoods tend to have less access to quality schools, health care, and decent housing and face other detrimental conditions (Anderson, 1999; Noguera, 2003). Schools located in impoverished neighborhoods tend to be underfunded and overcrowded and to lack resources (Gottfredson, 2001). Not only does the lack of funding and resources reflect in part the tax bases of poorer communities, but also factors such as structural racism that divert funding from poorer schools and those with higher proportions of racially and ethnically marginalized youths (Morgan & Amerikaner, 2018). State and local government policies related to distribution of school funding, along with the educational and juvenile justice systems, often create and maintain disparities. Government policies (both formal and informal) that have served to concentrate poverty and create highly segregated communities are also implicated (e.g., Sampson & Wilson, 1995).

Gottfredson (2001) provided a complex theoretic framework in which she argues that multiple factors operate to help explain delinquency and other school outcomes for youth. In her model, community factors may impact school factors, which in turn may impact individual factors, and all three types of factors are associated with delinquency. For example, community factors associated with social disorganization theory (e.g., disorganization, poverty, high crime) may impact such factors as school overcrowding, student composition (e.g., heterogeneity, social class), and availability of drugs and weapons. The number of students impacts school administration management (e.g., discipline management, coordination of resources, communication) and organization of work (e.g., types of departments, specialization of teachers), both of which impact the communal social organization of schools (e.g., relationships between teachers, between teachers and students).

School climate in disorganized areas may have implications for student outcomes. Kirk (2009) sought to understand the roles of social controls for suspensions and arrests of youths at the individual, school, and neighborhood levels. Using data from 6th- and 8th-graders and their teachers from Chicago, Kirk found that students were more likely to self-report being arrested when their neighborhoods had low levels of collective efficacy (an index assessing trust of neighborhood residents and belief that neighbors would act if they saw problems in their neighborhood) combined with low levels of trust between students and teachers. Additionally, students were less likely to be suspended when their schools had higher levels of school collective efficacy (an index based on whether teachers trusted their peers and believed they would act to help students and the school), and this protective effect was especially strong when the schools were located in neighborhoods with low collective efficacy.

IMPLICATIONS AND CONCLUSION

As this chapter shows, there is great potential for criminology and education to work in interdisciplinary fashion, as the two disciplines have numerous points of overlapping interests. The move to greater use of zero-tolerance policies and exclusionary school discipline comes from broader tough-on-crime policies (e.g., Garland, 2001; Hirschfield, 2008, 2018; Morris & Perry, 2016) and is supported by federal government grants and policies. Both education scholars and criminologists are greatly interested in school violence and other misbehavior. Criminology is increasingly focused on implications of zero-tolerance policies and exclusionary school discipline, such as higher likelihood of arrests (Mowen & Brent, 2016; Wolf & Kupchik, 2017), with implications for future educational attainment (Hirschfield, 2009; Kirk & Sampson 2011, 2013; Sweeten et al., 2009), and thus for earnings potential and subsequent crime involvement. The two disciplines have many common concerns; nevertheless, there is little communication between them. Communication and interdisciplinary work would greatly benefit both education and criminology scholars.

In this chapter, three criminological theories—racial threat, labeling, and social disorganization—were used to provide theoretical frames for critically examining education policies and practices. Application of these three approaches to critically examine school policies, particularly related to discipline, show that zero-tolerance policies such as suspension and expulsion as well as arrests for school-related misbehaviors serve to create, maintain, and exacerbate inequities across groups. In this chapter, the focus has largely been on racial and ethnic inequities in educational attainment and use of school discipline, but other sites (e.g., special education) are also clearly implicated (U.S. Department of Education, Office for Civil Rights, 2019).

Consistent with the IBA frame (see p. 3, Table I.1, this volume), we thus see that education and the juvenile and criminal justice systems, along with government policies, are key systems/locations of overlap with critical implications for individual youths and their outcomes and futures. Specifically, related to IBA question 1, "How do existing policies and practices address, maintain or create inequities between different groups?," educational and juvenile justice/criminal justice policies clearly maintain and create inequities. They do so by impacting educational access and the school environment, and by increasing the likelihood that students will have contact with the juvenile or criminal justice system; thus these policies have long-term implications for life chances. Concerning IBA question 2, "How are groups differentially affected (privileged/oppressed) by this representation of the problem?": All students and young people are impacted. However, racially and ethnically marginalized students, poorer students, and students in special education are particularly disadvantaged due to these policies and practices. Related to IBA question 3, "Which are the important intersecting social locations and systems?," three are key: educational policy and the juvenile and criminal justice systems. Funding, grant policies, and the tough-on-crime approach—all are implicated in the maintenance of inequities.

The intersections between education and criminology, including through some of the processes addressed via these criminological frames, serve as sites of oppression for some youths, especially those racially and ethnically minoritized, and certainly have implications for their futures. This is especially true for youths who reside in and attend schools located in disadvantaged, disorganized communities. As such, not only do education and criminology overlap, but considering both disciplines allows for a broader lens through which to view some of the key issues of relevance to both.

The brief overview of these issues in this chapter suggests several needed policy changes to reduce inequities the policies have created and maintained. The use of exclusionary school discipline needs to be reduced dramatically. While students who are violent and interfere with or impact the well-being and learning opportunities of other youth should face sanctions, suspension and expulsion should be reserved for the most problematic of youth behavior (Kirk & Sampson, 2011). Moreover, rather than just suspending or expelling the youths, greater efforts should be made to identify and address the source of misbehavior (Bowditch, 1993; Kupchik, 2009; Na & Gottfredson, 2013). Similarly, while SROs in schools are now widespread, arrest and referral to law enforcement should be reserved for the most serious transgressions. These suggestions are intended to reduce the detrimental impacts of suspension, expulsion, and arrest on the youths themselves as well as on the school environment more broadly.

In addition, schools should seek to adopt or more broadly incorporate restorative or reintegrative practices (e.g., mediation) (Payne & Welch 2010, 2015). This should diminish the harmful effects of exclusionary and zero-tolerance punishments for youths. When students are sanctioned, efforts should be made to reintegrate them into good standing in the school, rather than to have the punishment serve as their primary identity, subjecting them to labeling processes from teachers, administrators, and peers (e.g., Braithwaite, 1989; Wiley et al., 2013). This may further reduce the long-term implications of labeling addressed here. Disproportionate use of zero-tolerance policies in schools that have large populations of students of color (per discussion of racial threat theory) needs further examination. Extensive use of such policies is not only harmful overall but also sets the stage for students of color in particular to be subject to harsh discipline and its resultant problems. Fundamentally, this maintains and exacerbates disparities across racial and ethnic groups in terms of educational attainment and juvenile justice and criminal justice involvement, and has critical implications for long-term life chances and (more broadly) societal well-being and social justice (e.g., Kirk & Sampson, 2011, 2013; Kupchik, 2016).

REFERENCES

Anderson, E. (1999). *Code of the street: Decency, violence, and the moral life of the inner city.* W. W. Norton.

Agnew, R. (2006). *Pressured into crime: An overview of general strain theory.* Roxbury Publishers.

Bernburg, J. G., & Krohn, M. D. (2003). Labeling, life chances, and adult crime: The direct and indirect effects of official intervention in adolescence on crime in early adulthood. *Criminology, 41,* 1287–1318.

Bernburg, J. G., Krohn, M.D., & Rivera, C. J. (2006). Official labeling, criminal embeddedness, and subsequent delinquency: A longitudinal test of labeling theory. *Journal of Research in Crime and Delinquency, 43,* 67–88.

Blalock, H. (1967). *Towards a theory of minority group relations.* Capricorn Books.

Blumer, H. (1958). Race prejudice as a sense of group position. *The Pacific Sociological Review 1,* 3–7.

Bowditch, C. (1993). Getting rid of troublemakers: High school disciplinary procedures and the production of dropouts. *Social Problems, 40,* 493–509.

Braithwaite, J. (1989). *Crime, shame and reintegration.* Cambridge University Press.

Cavanagh, C., Nielsen, A. L., & Villarruel, F. A. (2019). Juvenile (in) justice: A system developed to facilitate youth development that challenges healthy outcomes. In H. Fitzgerald, D. J. Johnson, D. B. Qin, F. A. Villarruel, & J. Norder (Eds.), *Handbook of children and prejudice* (pp. 421–446). Springer Nature.

Duran, R. J. (2013). *Gang life in two cities: An insider's journey.* Columbia University Press.

Garland, D. (2001). *The culture of control: Crime and social order in contemporary society.* University of Chicago Press.

Gottfredson, D. C. (2001). *Schools and delinquency.* Cambridge University Press.

Gottfredson, M. R., & Hirschi, T. (1990). *A general theory of crime.* Stanford University Press.

Hankivsky, O., Grace, D., Hunting, G., Giesbrecht, M., Fridkin, A., Rudrum, S., Ferlatte, O., & Clark, N. (2014). An intersectionality-based policy analysis framework: Critical reflections on a methodology for advancing equity. *International Journal for Equity in Health 13,* 119.

Hirschfield, P. J. (2008). Preparing for prison? The criminalization of school discipline in the USA. *Theoretical Criminology, 12,* 79–101.

Hirschfield, P. J. (2009). Another way out: The impact of juvenile arrests on high school dropout. *Sociology of Education, 82,* 368–393.

Hirschfield, P. J. (2018). Schools and crime. *Annual Review of Criminology 1,* 149–169.

Hirschfield, P. J., & Celinska, K. (2011). Beyond fear: Sociological perspectives on the criminalization of school discipline. *Sociology Compass, 5,* 1–12.

Hirschi, T. (1969). *Causes of delinquency.* University of California Press.

Hughes, C., Warren, P. Y., Stewart, E. A., Tomaskovic-Devey, D., & Mears, D. P. (2017). Racial threat, intergroup contact, and school punishment. *Journal of Research in Crime and Delinquency 54*(4), 583–616.

Jacobs, D., & Carmichael, J. T. (2001). The politics of punishment across time and space: A pooled time series analysis of imprisonment rates. *Social Forces, 80*(1), 61–91.

Jacobs, D., & Carmichael, J. T. (2002). The political sociology of the death penalty: A pooled time series analysis. *American Sociological Review, 109*(1), 109–131.

Jacobsen, W. C., Pace, G. T., & Ramirez, N. G. (2019). Punishment and inequality at an early age: Exclusionary discipline in elementary school. *Social Forces, 97*(3), 973–998.

Katz, S. R. (1997). Presumed guilty: How schools criminalize Latino youth. *Social Justice, 24*, 77–95.

Keen, B., & Jacobs, D. (2009). Racial threat, partisan politics, and racial disparities in prison admissions: A panel analysis. *Criminology, 47*(1), 209–238.

Kent, S. L., & Jacobs, D. (2005). Minority threat and police strength from 1980 to 2000: A fixed effects analysis of nonlinear and interactive effects in large U.S. cities. *Criminology, 43*, 731–760.

Kirk, D. S. (2009). Unraveling the contextual effects of student suspension and juvenile arrest: The independent and interdependent influences of school, neighborhood, and family social controls. *Criminology, 47*(2), 479–520.

Kirk, D. S., & Sampson, R. J. (2011). Crime and the production of safe schools. In G. J. Duncan & R. J. Murnane (Eds.). *Whither opportunity?: Rising inequality, schools, and children's life chances* (pp. 397–417). Russell Sage Foundation.

Kirk, D. S., & Sampson, R. J. (2013). Juvenile arrest and collateral educational damage in the transition to adulthood. *Sociology of Education, 86*(1), 36–62.

Kupchik, A. (2009). Things are tough all over: Race, ethnicity, class and school discipline. *Punishment & Society, 11*, 291–317.

Kupchik, A. (2016). *The real school safety problem: The long-term consequences of harsh school punishment.* University of California Press.

Kupchik, A., & Ward, G. (2013). Race, poverty, and exclusionary school security: An empirical analysis of U.S. elementary, middle, and high schools. *Youth Violence and Juvenile Justice, 12*, 332–354.

Lemert, E.M. (1951). *Social pathology: A systematic approach to the theory of sociopathic behavior.* McGraw-Hill.

Matsueda, R. L. (1992). Reflected appraisals, parental labeling, and delinquency: Specifying a symbolic interactionist theory. *American Journal of Sociology, 97*, 1577–1611.

Moffitt, T. (1993). Adolescence-limited and life-course-persistent anti-social behavior: A developmental taxonomy. *Psychological Review, 100*(4), 674–701.

Morgan, I., & Amerikaner, A. (2018). *Funding gaps 2018: An analysis of school funding equity across the U.S. and within each state.* Education Trust. https://files.eric.ed.gov/fulltext/ED587198.pdf

Morris, E.W. (2005). "Tuck in that shirt!" Race, class, gender, and discipline in an urban school. *Sociological Perspectives, 48*(1), 25–48.

Morris, E.W., & Perry, B.L. (2016). The punishment gap: School suspension and racial disparities in achievement. *Social Problems, 63*, 68–86.

Morris, E.W., & Perry, B.L. (2017). Girls behaving badly? Race, gender, and subjective evaluation in the discipline of African American girls. *Sociology of Education, 90*(2), 127–148.

Mowen, T. J., & Brent, J. (2016). School discipline as a turning point: The cumulative effect of suspension on arrest. *Journal of Research in Crime and Delinquency, 53*, 628–653.

Mowen, T. J., Brent, J. J., & Bowman, J. H., IV. (2019). The effect of school discipline on offending across time. *Justice Quarterly, 37*(4), 737–760. https://doi.org/10.1080/07418825.2019.1625428

Na, C., & Gottfredson, D. C. (2013). Police officers in schools: Effects on school crime and the processing of offending behaviors. *Justice Quarterly, 30*(4), 619–650.

Nicholson-Crotty, S., Birchmeier, Z., & Valentine, D. (2009). Exploring the impact of school discipline on racial disproportion in the juvenile justice system. *Social Science Quarterly, 90*, 1003–1018.

Noguera, P. A. (2003). The trouble with Black boys: The role and influence of environmental and cultural factors on the academic performance of African American males. *Urban Education, 38*(4), 431–459.

Owens, E. G. (2017). Testing the school-to-prison pipeline. *Journal of Public Policy Analysis and Management, 36*(1), 11–37.

Owens, J., & McLanahan, S. S. (2020). Unpacking the drivers of racial disparities in school suspension and expulsion. *Social Forces*, 98, 1548–1577.

Padilla, F. M. (1993). *The gang as an American enterprise.* Rutgers University Press.

Payne, A. A., & Welch, K. (2010). Modeling the effects of racial threat on punitive and restorative school discipline practices. *Criminology 48*(4), 1019–1062.

Payne, A. A., & Welch, K. (2015). Restorative justice in schools: The influence of race on restorative discipline. *Youth & Society 47*(4), 539–564.

Peguero, A. A., & Shekarkhar, Z. (2011). Latino/a student misbehavior and school punishment. *Hispanic Journal of Behavioral Sciences, 33*(1), 54–70.

Perry, B. L., & Morris, E. W. (2014). Suspending progress: Collateral consequences of exclusionary punishment in public schools. *American Sociological Review, 79*(6), 1067–1087.

Pettit, B., & Western, B. (2004). Mass imprisonment and the life course: Race and class inequality in U.S. incarceration. *American Sociological Review, 69*(2), 151–169.

Rios, V. (2011). *Punished: Policing the lives of Black and Latino boys.* New York University Press.

Rocque, M., & Paternoster, R. (2011). Understanding the antecedents of the "school-to-jail" link: The relationship between race and school discipline. *Journal of Criminal Law & Criminology, 101*(2), 633–665.

Rodriguez, L. J. (2005). *Always running: La vida loca: Gang days in L.A.* Touchstone.

Rosenbloom, S. R., & Way, N. (2004). Experiences of discrimination among African American, Asian American, and Latino adolescents in an urban high school. *Youth & Society, 35*(4), 420–451.

Sampson, R. J. (2012). *Great American city: Chicago and the enduring neighborhood effect.* University of Chicago Press.

Sampson, R. J., Morenoff, J. D., & Gannon-Rowley, T. (2002). Assessing 'neighborhood effects': Social processes and new directions in research. *Annual Review of Sociology, 28*, 443–478.

Sampson, R. J., Raudenbush, S. W., & Earls, F. (1997). Neighborhoods and violent crime: A multilevel study of collective efficacy. *Science, 277*(5328), 918–924.

Sampson, R. J., & Wilson, W. J. (1995). Toward a theory of race, crime, and inequality. In J. Hagan & R.D. Peterson (Eds.), *Crime and inequality* (pp. 37–54). Stanford University Press.

Shaw, C. R., & McKay, H. D. (1969). *Juvenile delinquency and urban areas* (Rev. ed.). University of Chicago Press.

Simon, J. (2009). *Governing through crime: How the war on crime transformed American democracy and created a culture of fear*. Oxford University Press.

Skiba, R. J., Horner, R. H., Chung, C., Rausch, M. K., May, S. L., & Tobin, T. (2011). Race is not neutral: A national investigation of African American and Latinx disproportionality in school discipline. *School Psychology Review, 40*(1), 85–107.

Skiba, R. J., Michael, R. S., Nardo, A. C., & Peterson, R. L. (2002). The color of discipline: Sources of racial and gender disproportionality in school punishment. *The Urban Review, 34*(4), 317–342.

Snipes, J. B., Bernard, T. J., & Gerould, A. L. (2019). *Vold's theoretical criminology* (8th ed.). Oxford University Press.

Sweeten, G., Bushway, S.D., & Paternoster, R. (2009). Does dropping out of school mean dropping into delinquency? *Criminology, 47*(1), 47–92.

U.S. Department of Education, Office for Civil Rights. (2019). *School climate and safety: 2015–16 civil rights data collection*. https://www2.ed.gov/about/offices /list/ocr/docs/ school-climate-and-safety.pdf

Welch, K., & Payne, A. A. (2010). Racial threat and punitive school discipline. *Social Problems, 57*(1), 25–48.

Welch, K., & Payne, A. A. (2012). Exclusionary school punishment: The effect of racial threat on expulsion and suspension. *Youth Violence and Juvenile Justice 10*(2), 155–171.

Western, B. (2002). The impact of incarceration on wage mobility and inequality. *American Sociological Review, 67*(4), 526–546.

Wiley, S. A., Slocum, L. A., & Esbensen, F. A. (2013). The unintended consequences of being stopped or arrested: An exploration of the labeling mechanisms through which police contact leads to subsequent delinquency. *Criminology, 51*(4), 927–966.

Wolf, K. C., & Kupchik, A. (2017). School suspensions and adverse experiences in adulthood. *Justice Quarterly, 34*(3), 407–430.

Wright, J. P., Morgan, M. A., Coyne, M. A., Beaver, K. M., & Barnes, J. C. (2014). Prior problem behavior accounts for the racial gap in school suspensions. *Journal of Criminal Justice, 42*(3), 257–266.

Part II

APPLICATIONS OF INTERSECTIONALITY-BASED ANALYSIS FRAMEWORKS AND POLICIES

Toward More Effective Policy, Practice, and Research in Child Welfare and Education

Kele Stewart and Wendy Cavendish

Students in the foster care system are among the most academically vulnerable in schools because of their intersecting marginalized social identities and overlapping negative experiences with interlocking systems. There are approximately 423,997 children in foster care, including 264,579 school-aged children (U.S. Department of Health and Human Services, 2020). While it has been well documented that race/ethnicity and socioeconomic status are significant indicators of achievement for Black and Latinx students (Duncan & Magnuson, 2011), there is also an achievement gap for students in foster care that has received less research and policy attention (Smithgall et al., 2004). Students from minoritized, low-income, and foster care backgrounds have lower rates of high school graduation and college matriculation and completion, and poorer outcomes on other academic measures, than their peers (Smithgall et al., 2004; Snyder, 2018). Preliminary studies suggest that students in foster care may experience even greater school challenges than other marginalized youth (Piescher et al., 2014), and that children of color in foster care are even more at risk for failure than the general population of foster youth (Ryan et al., 2008). The persistence of these gaps suggests minimal progress toward educational equity, despite policy efforts to provide equal opportunities to low-income minority students (Barton & Coley, 2010) and to address child welfare and education system barriers to educational opportunity for children in foster care (Stewart & Thorrington, 2019). The terms *foster care system* and *child welfare system* are used interchangeably in this chapter to refer to the group of public and private services that provide investigation, intervention, and treatment to children and families when child maltreatment occurs. *Foster care* refers to an array of placements and services when the risk to the child warrants removal from the parent or primary caregivers' home, and may include placements with relatives, foster homes, or group care.

An equity-focused intersectionality-based analysis (IBA) approach offers a promising opportunity to conduct research and policy analysis that informs more just and effective policies to address the multiple layers of marginalization faced by students in foster care. Intersectionality teaches that "students, their families and their communities live multiple, layered identities derived from social relations, history and the operation of structures of power and that they are exposed to different types of discrimination and disadvantage that occur as a consequence of the combination of identities" (McIntosh, 2019, para. 2). Children in foster care may have multiple marginalized identities that shape their experiences (Wilson et al., 2014). The goal of intersectionality-based research and policy analysis is to identify and address the way specific policy approaches address these inequalities, taking into account that social identities interact to form unique meanings and complex experiences within and between groups (Hankivsky & Cormier, 2011).

Children in foster care also live at the intersection of two systems—education and child welfare—that independently produce disparate outcomes based on social identities, and overlap in ways that contribute to these students' negative educational trajectory. Each system implements seemingly neutral policies and practices that often obfuscate the role of social identities. An intersectionality-based approach provides the opportunity to explore what or who is obscured when policies are applied across students with different social identities (Harris & Leonardo, 2018). IBA also provides the opportunity to conduct research and develop interventions that account for and seek to reduce inequities.

Some researchers have used an intersectional lens to demonstrate ways in which the educational system systematically alienates, punishes, and ultimately pushes out students based on intersections of race, class, gender, sexual orientation, and disability (McIntosh, 2019). There is, however, limited research on successful interventions to address the educational needs of children in foster care, and even fewer studies that account for the experiences and structural context of multiply marginalized foster youth who are impacted by both the child welfare and education systems. This chapter seeks to fill this gap by applying IBA to make visible the intersecting social locations, systems, and policies contributing to the experiences of students in the foster care system and sharing a research model exemplar for multidimensional exploration of the link between the micro experiences of youth in foster care and the social institutions seeking to meet their needs.

INTERSECTIONALITY AND FOSTER YOUTH
IN THE CHILD WELFARE SYSTEM

The child welfare system is the complex legal, administrative, and social service response to child maltreatment by caregivers. All states require designated professionals, including teachers and school personnel, to report suspected maltreatment, while some state reporting laws are even broader, requiring anyone suspecting maltreatment to make reports. Following an investigation, the Child Protective Service (CPS) agency determines whether the allegations are substantiated and decides whether the child can remain safely at home or should be removed from the home. If the child is removed, CPS typically becomes the child's legal custodian and the child may be temporarily placed in a variety of settings, including with relatives and fictive kin, or in foster homes and group homes.

Social identities based on race, class, ethnicity, ability, sexual orientation, and gender disproportionately determine who ends up in the child welfare system (Fluke et al., 2011; National Council on Disability, 2008; Wilson et al., 2014). There is overrepresentation of Black, Native American, and low-income children in the foster care system (Miller et al., 2014; Summers, 2015). While Latinx children are slightly underrepresented nationally, they are overrepresented in several states (Ganasarajah et al., 2017). There is also overrepresentation of LGBTQ children and children with disabilities (National Council on Disability, 2008). These youth have multiple identities. For example, one study of LGBTQ youth aging out of foster care in Los Angeles found that the majority were youth of color (Wilson et al., 2014). While exploration of the complex reasons for overrepresentation are beyond the scope of this chapter, they include factors such as concentrated poverty and structural racism, bias among child welfare and external actors, and the disparate impact of child welfare policies and practices on children from marginalized backgrounds (Fluke et al., 2011).

Studies show that racial disparities also occur at multiple decision points in the child welfare system, including investigation, removal, and exit from the system (Font, 2013; Putnam-Hornstein et al., 2013). While in foster care, marginalized youth also experience disparate treatment and inequitable delivery of services like placements, mental health treatment, and medical care (Fluke et. al., 2011; Wilson et. al., 2014). In addition to poor schooling outcomes, children who age out of foster care experience poor outcomes in adulthood, including low college matriculation and graduation rates and higher rates of homelessness, unemployment, and incarceration (e.g., Dworsky & Perez, 2010). And these outcomes occur disproportionately for youth of color, who are more likely to age out of foster care.

Policy Challenges in Child Welfare

This section highlights examples of child welfare policies and practices that impede the emotional well-being and academic progress of foster care students, contributing to disparate experiences and outcomes based on social identity. Studies have identified several factors that contribute to poor educational outcomes for youth in foster care, including high school mobility and related disruption in education or loss of credits and records in school transfers; trauma and behavioral problems; lack of communication between the school and child welfare system; and lack of parental advocates (Ferguson & Wolkow, 2012; Noonan et al., 2012). Below, we contextualize these factors through an intersectional lens to reveal the significance of structural interactions with social identities.

Removal of children from their families and speedy termination of parental rights if parents fail to comply with court-ordered reunification plans are among the child welfare policies that, scholars and advocates argue, most disadvantage children of color and low-income families (Roberts, 1999). The vast majority of child welfare cases are for neglect, which focuses on a parent's inability to meet their child's basic needs, such as food, shelter, and access to medical care. Vague state neglect laws are applied in ways that conflate neglect with poverty (Pimentel, 2019). Children of color are removed from their homes at disproportional rates (Fluke et. al., 2011), and removal is itself a traumatic event that has long-term psychological consequences (Bell, 2016).

The Adoption and Safe Families Act (ASFA, 1997) prioritizes swift family reunification and terminates parental rights for children who have been in care for 15 out of 22 months, while simultaneously incentivizing adoption. This has also contributed to disparate outcomes for children of color. The speed and quality of services impacts successful reunification, and there is evidence of inequitable distribution of resources and services to children and families including housing, mental health treatment, and child care (Fluke et al., 2011). Children of color are less likely to be reunified with family, even when controlling for risk factors, child behavior, or agency actions (Dunbar & Barth, 2007). Children of color are also less likely to be adopted and more likely to age out of care (Fluke et al., 2011). The result is that many children of color in foster care (with intersecting social identities) are disconnected from family and extended support networks, and their foster care experiences have significant developmental, emotional, and psychological effects (Riebschleger et al., 2015).

For marginalized youth, the trauma that prompted state intervention is often exacerbated by longer stays in foster care, frequent placement changes, more restrictive placements, and inadequate mental health and other services (Fluke et al., 2011). Placement instability, which is more likely to occur the longer youth are in foster care, is associated with social, behavioral, and academic problems (Konjin et al., 2019). In general, placement instability is high among foster youth (Konjin et al., 2019), and even higher for foster youth of color and LGBTQ foster youth (Wilson et al., 2014). These frequent home changes often lead to school changes or disruption, a significant factor in poor academic outcomes for foster youth (Clemens & Sheesley, 2016).

When children in foster care display behavioral problems, symptoms of trauma, or norm-violating behavior, they are often labeled as troublesome, hostile, or pathological (Miller et al., 2014; Weithorn, 2005). These are children who may not have severe mental health disorders, but for whom the policy response is often punitive and extreme, such as psychotropic medication, placement in a locked psychiatric facility, or juvenile justice involvement (Weithorn, 2005). In a practical example, the Florida legislature considered a proposal to place children who had refused a placement offered by the Child Protective Service agency into a secure juvenile detention center (O'Donnell, 2019). Although race was never discussed in the policy debate, a study revealed that the children at issue in the proposal were overwhelmingly youth of color who had, as a group, experienced a median of 21 placements (Latham, 2019). It is critical that policies designed to address issues like placement and school instability consider the differential impact on marginalized and multiply marginalized youth.

INTERSECTIONALITY AND FOSTER YOUTH IN THE SCHOOL SYSTEM

Race and socioeconomic class are among the most significant indicators of school standardized test scores, graduation rates, and other educational measures. Families of color are disproportionately concentrated in impoverished urban neighborhoods with underperforming schools (Reardon et al., 2019). Even controlling for geography and class, race has been theorized as a salient factor in understanding inequities in the education system (Ladson-Billings & Tate, 1995). With race as a central factor, special education and school discipline are among the structural mechanisms that contribute to poor academic outcomes. Students in special education and with school discipline records, groups that overlap substantially, are less likely to graduate and matriculate to higher education, and more likely to be funneled into the school-to-prison pipeline (Heitzig, 2016).

Children in foster care are generally overrepresented in special education. An estimated 30% to 50% of children in foster care receive special education services, compared with 14% among students overall (U.S. Department of Education, 2019; Zetlin et al., 2012). One study noted that children in foster care with disabilities had poorer academic outcomes than children in foster care only, and they were placed in more restrictive school settings than most children in special education (Geenan & Powers, 2006). This suggests that the impact of being in both foster care and special education has a negative multiplier effect. O'Higgins and colleagues (2017) conducted a systematic review across a 26-year period on factors associated with educational outcomes for children in foster and kinship care. They concluded that male gender, ethnic minority status, and special education status consistently predicted poor educational outcomes.

Challenges in Special Education Policy

This section focuses on special education policy as an example of a structural mechanism that plays a role in disparate outcomes for children of color, children with disabilities, and among foster youth. This is important because bias in referrals and school system processes that label students as disabled or disruptive is one step in a process likely to lead to dropping out and to juvenile justice involvement (Cavendish et al., 2014). While the relationships among special education placement, discipline policies, and juvenile justice involvement have been studied and theorized, there has been limited focus on the relationship among these policies as enacted in schools and the experiences of youth in foster care.

The Individuals with Disabilities Education Improvement Act (IDEA, 2004) provides protections for students identified with a disability and guarantees students with disabilities a free and appropriate public education in the least restrictive setting. While IDEA provisions require individualized services (such as those provided through Individualized Education Plans [IEPs]) for children with disabilities and guarantee procedural protections to children and families, "the benefits of special education have not been equitably distributed on the basis of race and social class" (Blanchett, 2009, p. 378). Over half of youth with IEPs are from low-SES households (Liu et al., 2018), and a disproportionate number of Black students are referred for special education services and isolated in separate classrooms (Artiles et al., 2016).

Black students are also more than twice as likely to be labeled with an Emotional Behavior Disorder (EBD) compared with their White peers. This label often creates a stigma that has long-term effects on higher education and employment prospects (Mandell et al., 2008). Among the overall student population receiving special education services, about 5% of students qualified under the category of Emotional and Behavioral Disorders (U.S. Department of Education, 2019). In contrast, approximately 50% of children in foster care who are enrolled in special education have identified emotional or behavioral disorders (Zetlin et al., 2012).

Parental involvement in special education presents another challenge. The IDEA (2004) specifies that parents are to be considered equal partners in the educational planning process (e.g., Landmark et al., 2013). However, much of the research on parent involvement in special education reveals that parents report significant challenges to participation in IEP meetings. The barriers reported have included lack of opportunity for input, communication and/or language challenges, and deficit views expressed by the school and its agents whereby parents noted feelings of alienation (e.g., Valle, 2009), as well as feeling coerced into signing documents that they did not fully understand (Tucker & Schwartz, 2013; Valle & Aponte, 2002; Zeitlin & Curcic, 2014).

Parental advocacy is often missing in the lives of children in foster care. Research shows that children in foster care may not have someone at IEP meetings (Hill, 2013). Children at the intersection of child welfare and education are often not living with their biological parents, and there may be confusion as to who has legal rights, or there may be so many professionals in the child's life that responsibility is diffused. Thus, there is often a disconnect between the intent of the parent involvement provisions of IDEA and the actual implementation for foster youth.

BRINGING AN INTERSECTIONAL LENS TO POLICIES TO ADDRESS THE EDUCATIONAL NEEDS OF CHILDREN IN FOSTER CARE

There is a lack of research related to the intersectional needs of youth in foster care that includes a consideration of both foster care and education systems and contexts. There is therefore a need to critically examine how policies and programs targeted to youth in foster care consider or include the unique structural experiences of these multiply marginalized youth. Policies (such as the Every Student Succeeds Act of 2015) targeted at improving educational outcomes for children in foster care have focused on improving interagency communication and collaboration between the child welfare and education systems, minimizing school changes and the disruptive impact when changes do occur, and appointing surrogate parents for children in special education proceedings. While these considerations are necessary, a broader examination of the full educational experience of foster care youth would be beneficial. Viewed through an intersectionality lens, current policy analysis and research do not account for the complex intersections between social identity and the powerful forces within both foster care and education systems that do not provide opportunities for students to meet their potential.

The Every Student Succeeds Act (ESSA, 2015) was the first major piece of federal education legislation to explicitly address the education of children in foster care. ESSA requires local education agencies (school districts) to ensure that foster youth be enrolled or remain in their school of origin, unless it is not in their best interests. It also requires schools and child welfare agencies to enter agreements to coordinate transportation to allow students to remain in their school of origin. This provision matched a similar school stability provision in federal child welfare law (Fostering Connections to Success, 2008). This represents a sound policy shift grounded in research showing the link between school mobility and loss of academic learning time. But we do not yet have data showing whether these policies are being implemented and, if they are, that they are effective. Nor are there standards or assessments to determine whether school decisions are in fact in the child's best interests. Thus we do not have sufficient information to understand how this policy might improve the schooling experience of multiply marginalized youth confronting the structural barriers described in this chapter.

ESSA also requires state and local education agencies (SEAs and LEAs) to appoint a liaison to the child welfare system. Despite the overlap in children served, the two systems (child welfare and education) often do not communicate or collaborate with each other. The very limited information available about implementation of liaison positions suggests that while the liaison role appears to facilitate some communication and opportunities to problem-solve issues for children in care, there have been inconsistent implementation and role definition and continued barriers to effective collaboration and communication (Shea et al., 2010; Stewart & Thorrington, 2019). And we have no information about whether the liaison focuses on or is equipped to address the micro and macro challenges confronting multiply marginalized youth.

As noted, although challenges to the facilitation of meaningful parental involvement in special education planning required by IDEA provisions have been robustly reported, foster youth face additional obstacles to meaningful parent involvement in IEP meetings. To account for the fact that the biological parents of children in foster care may not be able to be fully involved in IEP development and implementation planning in IEP meetings, IDEA allows foster parents and other caregivers to serve as parents for purposes of IDEA. IDEA also allows courts or school systems to appoint a surrogate parent to act on children's behalf. These policies are well-intentioned but will not make a difference unless we account for the ways in which child welfare and school system policies collude in creating the environment for continued failure of multiply marginalized children (Blanchett, 2009).

POLICY CONSIDERATIONS IN CROSS-DISCIPLINARY RESEARCH

The policy context must be considered in meaningful research that examines the lived experience and context within and across systems for foster youth. In the final section of this chapter, we share an example of research with and for foster youth that is also built upon the acknowledgement of cross-system policy gaps.

The First Star Academy research project is a project in which we applied the IBA framework to a longitudinal research design and analysis of an education-related transition support intervention program for middle and high school youth in the child welfare system. An intersectional lens provided our guiding framework at all levels of the program and research development, from inception (the design of the program), to conception (design of the study), to intervention and analysis (ongoing analysis into the problem) (Hankivsky & Cormier, 2011; Harris & Leonardo, 2018). Singular analytical approaches fall short of the complexity needed to examine multiple sites of oppression legitimated in schools and the foster care system (Carey et al., 2015); thus, we spent the better part of a year planning the mixed method design and analytic plan that would speak to this complexity (Harris & Leonardo, 2018).

The overarching goal of First Star Academy is to ensure that the foster youth participants (N = 48) graduate from high school with the necessary skills and have access to resources to successfully transition to postsecondary education and/or sustained employment. The research team developed a Theory of Change (ToC) framework for the project that focused on the multidimensional and cross-system experiences of youth. The Theory of Change framework for the project is provided in Figure 4.1.

The overarching goal of our project outlined in the ToC framework is to ensure that the foster youth participants graduate from high school with the skills and knowledge of resources that will allow them to successfully transition to post-secondary education or employment. This goal is supported by each of the steps in the pathways of self-determination development, academic success, interpersonal and life skills, career preparation, advocacy skills, and caregiver support. The ToC framework depicted in the figure is a graphic representation of the First Star Academy project's outcomes for each pathway, with included intervention strategies or activities to support development in each pathway within the diagram. Importantly, the ToC is framed through backwards mapping of pathways with the intended outcome listed at the top and, below that, each precondition or step that is needed to achieve the outcome. The outcomes are listed at the top of each pathway related to self-determination; academic success; social, interpersonal, and life skills; career preparation; advocacy; and caregiver support.

Figure 4.1. Theory of Change Framework

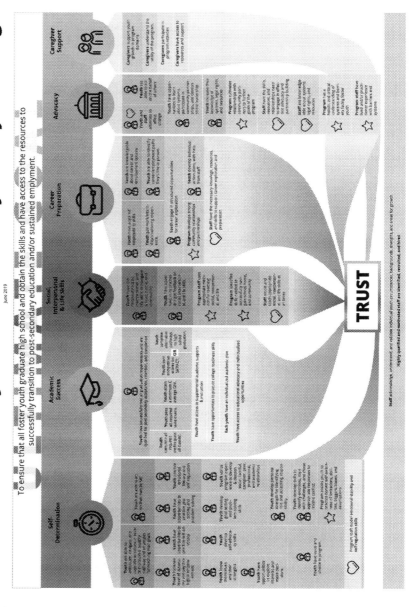

First Star University of Miami Academy Theory of Change

Every item in the figure represents a data source collected over the 4 years of the project.

In our Theory of Change framework, we center the perspectives and experiences of the youth both within the program as well as related to practices and data across both systems (child welfare and education). Further, we recognize that the youths' experiences and interactions in the child welfare and education systems cannot be separated from the historic structural racism that undergirds those systems.

APPLICATION OF IBA TO RESEARCH AND POLICY ANALYSIS

Youth in foster care must navigate the intersection of two systems—education and child welfare. As noted in this chapter, each system enacts policies with intent to increase equity, but the implementation of these policies in practice do not often lead to improved experiences or greater equity in outcomes for youth of color and/or youth served in special education in foster care. Because there is limited research on interventions that consider the experiences and structural context of multiply marginalized foster youth, we share our approach in using an intersectionality-based research design based on IBA that also considers the impact of policy approaches as experienced by foster youth themselves.

In Table 4.1 we provide a description of the First Star Academy research project details and data as they pertain to both the research and policy analysis (IBA) guiding questions.

Our hope is that this approach to conducting research and policy analysis leads to more equitable outcomes for the foster youth in the First Star Academy program, and also that the centering of the experiences and perspectives of youth as they move to adulthood will empower them as collaborators with researchers and policymakers, so as to inform policies and practices that can address the multiple layers of marginalization faced by youth at the intersection of child welfare and education systems built on the foundation of structural racism.

Table 4.1. Application of Intersectionality-Based Analysis Guiding Questions

Intersectionality-Based Analysis (IBA) Guiding Questions	IBA in First Star Academy
What knowledge, values, and experiences do you bring to this area of policy or practice? What social determinants (race, gender, class, citizenship etc.) affect your perspective?	This project represents a cross-disciplinary collaboration between researchers and practitioners in Law and Education. Kelé Stewart is a Black female immigrant law school professor whose legal clinic advocates on behalf of youth in foster care and whose academic research focuses on child welfare policy, including the intersection of education and child welfare. Wendy Cavendish is a White female former teacher and current education professor with experience working with diverse, urban schools, teachers, students, and families to facilitate more equitable outcomes for marginalized students.

The project graduate student research team includes a Latinx former foster youth with extensive nonprofit agency experience, a Black former high school teacher, and a Latinx special education teacher. |
Policy & Practice	
How do existing policies and practices address, maintain, or create inequities between different groups? Which are the important intersecting social locations and systems?	This project was designed by foregrounding the intersectional vulnerabilities of foster youth served in education. We identified the intersecting locations as schools and foster care placements and the systems as child welfare and education. As noted, while the education policies (IDEA and ESSA) include protections and/or provisions for foster youth, the systems do not work in tandem nor communicate with each other to provide supports for youth and families.
Who will be responsible (and who is best positioned) to ensure the implementation of the recommendations?	Built into the First Star Academy Theory of Change framework (see Figure 4.1) is a focus on the psychosocial development and support of youth that includes programming and data monitoring for self-determination skills (Ryan & Deci, 2017) with support for the development of self-advocacy and transformative social advocacy skills. This focus, coupled with the iterative developmental program evaluation process that includes youth input, is designed to facilitate youth and staff development as agents of change and advocates for others within the child welfare system.

Research	
Does the research advance the perspectives of those under study?	The First Star research project centers youth perspectives and experiences both within the program and across the child welfare and school systems. Our data sources include youth and staff surveys, focus groups, interview protocols, standardized measures for self-determination and social network development, and, importantly, individualized transition plans that include youth goals in the domains of education, independent living, social relationships, and employment/career exploration. All programming and adjustments to measures and data sources collected by the program and from the child welfare and school systems are driven by the goal areas identified by youth themselves on the transition plans.
Is the research framed within context? Does it reflect self-identified needs of affected groups/communities?	The research is framed within both the micro context (programmatically and youth-centered) and the larger school and child welfare system contexts. We have used a developmental approach for evaluation to monitor, document, and adapt the program relative to changing strengths and needs of the participants. This iterative process has been useful in the program's development and implementation, as we are focused on addressing complex and multilayered problems in real time. Because of its embeddedness in program design, the ongoing developmental evaluations have allowed us to essentially co-construct the program with the youth. This iterative process allows for an understanding of context and time-sensitive insights to inform program adaptations in response to both emergent findings and changing circumstances. We use a combination of qualitative and quantitative methods to investigate program process and youth outcomes.
Is the tool of inquiry suited to collecting micro or macro data, or a combination of both? How are interactions at individual levels of experience linked to social institutions and processes of power?	In this project, we collect both micro and macro data. The micro data include youth and staff perspectives, academic progress measures, psychosocial skill development (e.g., Self-determination Scale), and social network/social capital development (via Social Network Analysis). The macro sources include data from across both child welfare (placement changes and child welfare case notes and legal rulings) and school district systems (school mobility and attendance rates, school credits and grades, and state assessment scores). The interactions between youth experiences and progress and the practices and procedures in the education and child welfare systems are central to our analyses.

REFERENCES

Adoption and Safe Families Act, Pub. L. 105-89, 42 U.S.C. § 671 *et. seq.* (1997).

Artiles, A., Dorn, S., & Bal, A. (2016). Objects of protection, enduring nodes of difference: Disability intersections with "Other" differences, 1916–2016. *Review of Research in Education, 40*(1), 777–820.

Barton, P. E., & Coley, R. J. (2010). *The black-white achievement gap: When progress stopped.* Policy Information Report: Educational Testing Service.

Bell, W. (2016, October 24). *Keynote address.* Louisiana Partnership Annual Conference, Lafayette, LA. http://www.louisianapartnership.org

Blanchett, W. (2009). A retrospective examination of urban education: From Brown to resegregation of African Americans in special education—It is time to go for broke. *Urban Education, 44*(4), 370–388.

Carey, G., Malbon, E., Carey, N., Joyce, A., Crammond, B., & Carey, A. (2015). Systems science and systems thinking for public health: A systematic review of the field. *BMJ Open, 5*(12). http://dx.doi.org/10.1136/bmjopen-2015-009002

Cavendish, W., Artiles, A., & Harry, B. (2014). Tracking inequality 60 years after *Brown*: Does policy legitimize the racialization of disability? *Multiple Voices for Ethnically Diverse Exceptional Learners, 14*(2), 30–40.

Clemens, E. V., & Sheesley, A. P. (2016). Educational stability of Colorado's students in foster care: 2007–2008 to 2013–2014. http://www.unco.edu/cebs/foster-care-research/pdf/reports/Every_Transition_Counts_V.1_Interactive.pdf

Dunbar, K., & Barth, R. (2007). *Racial disproportionality, race disparity, and other race-related findings in published works derived from the National Survey of Child and Adolescent Well-Being.* Casey-CSP Alliance for Racial Equity. https://folio.iupui.edu/bitstream/handle/10244/134/Dunbar%20Barth%20Racial%20Disparity%20report%2012808.pdf?sequence=1

Duncan, G., & Magnuson, K. (2011). The nature and impact of early achievement skills, attention skills, and behavior problems. In G. Duncan & R. Murnane (Eds.), *Whither opportunity?: Rising inequality, schools, and children's life chances* (pp. 47–69). Russell Sage Foundation.

Dworsky, A., & Perez, A. (2010). Helping former foster youth graduate from college through campus support programs. *Children and Youth Services Review, 32*(2), 255–263. http:/doi.org/10.1016/j.childyouth.2009.09.004

Every Student Succeeds Act, Pub. L. 114-95, 20 U.S.C. 6301 *et. seq.* (2015).

Ferguson, H. B., & Wolkow, K. (2012). Educating children and youth in care: A review of barriers to school progress and strategies for change. *Children and Youth Services Review, 34*(6), 1143–1149. doi:10.1016/j.childyouth.2012.01.034

Fluke, J., Harden, B.J., Jenkins, M., & Ruehrdanz, A. (2011). Research synthesis on child welfare disproportionality and disparities. In Center for the Study of Social Policy and Annie E. Casey Foundation (Convenors), *Disparities and Disproportionality in Child Welfare: Analysis of the Research* [Symposium], (pp. 1–93). https://www.aecf.org/resources/disparities-and-disproportionality-in-child-welfare/

Font, S. A. (2013). Service referral patterns among Black and White families involved with child protective services. *Journal of Public Child Welfare, 7*(4), 370–391.

Fostering Connections to Success and Increasing Adoptions Act of 2008, P.L. 110-351,42 U.S.C. 675 *et seq.* (2008).

Ganasarajah, S., Siegel, G., & Sickmund, M. (2017). *Disproportionality rates for children of color in foster care (fiscal year 2015)*. National Council of Juvenile and Family Court Judges. https://www.ncjfcj.org/publications/disproportionality -rates-for-children-of-color-in-foster-care-fiscal-year-2015/

Geenan, S., & Powers, L. (2006). Are we ignoring youths with disabilities in foster care? An examination of their school performance. *Social Work, 51*(3), 233–41. doi:10.1093/sw/51.3.233

Hankivsky, O., & Cormier, R. (2011). Intersectionality and public policy: Some lessons from existing models. *Political Research Quarterly, 64*(1), 217–229.

Harris, A., & Leonardo, Z. (2018). Intersectionality, race-gender subordination and education. *Review of Research in Education, 42*(1), 1–27. https://doi .org/10.3102%2F0091732X18759071

Heitzig, N. (2016). *The school to prison pipeline: Education, discipline, and racialized double standards*. Praeger.

Hill, K. (2013). Special education experiences of older foster youth with disabilities: An analysis of state administrative data. *Journal of Public Child Welfare, 7*(5), 520–535.

Individuals with Disabilities Education Improvement Act 2004, P.L. 108-446, 20 U.S.C. § 1400 et seq., (2004).

Konjin, C., Admiraal, S., Baart, J., Rooij, F., Stams, G., Colonnesi, C., Lindauer, R., & Assink, M. (2019). Foster care placement instability: A meta-analytic review. *Children and Youth Services Review, 96*, 483–499.

Ladson-Billings, G., & Tate. W. F. (1995). Toward a Critical Race Theory of education. *Teachers College Record, 97*(1), 47–68.

Landmark, L., Roberts, B., & Zhang, D. (2013). Educators' beliefs and practices about parent involvement in transition planning. *Career Development and Transition for Exceptional Individuals, 36*(2), 114–123.

Latham, R. (2019). *A data study of youth who refused placements in Hillsborough county* [Report]. University of Miami School of Law, Children and Youth Law Clinic. https://miami.app.box.com/s/dipmi3w9su5j8u8m1fgp04daiceai1oq

Liu, A., Lacoe, J., Lipscomb, S., Haimson, J., Johnson, D.R., & Thurlow, M.L. (2018). *Preparing for life after high school: The characteristics and experiences of youth in special education*. National Center for Education Statistics, U.S. Department of Education. https://files.eric.ed.gov/fulltext/ED580934.pdf

Mandell, D., Davis, J., Bevans, K., & Guevara, J. (2008). Ethnic disparities in special education labeling among children with attention-deficit/hyperactivity disorder. *Journal of Emotional and Behavioral Disorders, 16*(1), 42–51.

McIntosh, L. M. (2019). Compound fractures: Healing the intersectionality of racism, classism and trauma in schools with a trauma-informed approach as part of a Social Justice Framework. *Journal of Educational Leadership and Policy Studies, 3*(1).

Miller, O., Farrow, F., Meltzer, J., & Notkin, S. (2014). *Changing course: Improving outcomes for African American males involved with child welfare systems*. Center for the Study of Social Policy. https://cssp.org/wp-content/uploads/2018 /08/Changing-Course_Improving-Outcomes-for-African-American-Males -Involved-with-Child-Welfare-Systems.pdf

National Council on Disability. (2008). *Youth with disabilities in the foster care system: Barriers to success and proposed policy solutions*. Author.

Noonan, K., Matone, M., Zlotnik, S., Hernandez-Mekonnen, R., Watts, C., Rubin, D., & Mollen, C. (2012). Cross-system barriers to educational success for children in foster care: The front line perspective. *Children and Youth Services Review, 34*(2), 403–408. https://doi.org/10.1016/j.childyouth.2011.11.006

O'Donnell, C. (2019, September 9). Problem foster kids could be locked up in 'secure' facility under new plan pushed by Tampa Bay child welfare agency. *Tampa Bay Times.* https://www.tampabay.com/news/hillsborough/2019/09/09 /problem-foster-kids-could-be-locked-up-in-secure-facility-under-new-plan -pushed-by-tampa-bay-child-welfare-agency/

O'Higgins, A., Sebba, J., & Gardner, F. (2017). What are the factors associated with educational achievement for children in kinship or foster care: A systematic review. *Children and Youth Services Review, 79*, 198–220. doi.org/10.1016/j .childyouth.2017.06.004

Piescher, K., Colburn, G., Laliberte, T., & Hong, S. (2014). Child protective services and the achievement gap. *Children and Youth Services Review, 47*(3), 408–415.

Pimental, D. (2019). Punishing families for being poor: How child protection interventions threaten the right to parent while impoverished. *Oklahoma Law Review, 71*(3), 885–921.

Putnam-Hornstein, E., Needell, B., King, B., & Johnson-Motoyama, M. (2013). Racial and ethnic disparities: A population-based examination of risk factors for involvement with child protective services. *Child Abuse & Neglect, 37*(1), 33–46.

Reardon, S. F., Weathers, E. S., Fahle, E. M., Jang, H., & Kalogrides, D. (2019). Is separate still unequal? New evidence on school segregation and racial academic achievement gaps (CEPA Working Paper No.19-06). Stanford Center for Education Policy Analysis. http://cepa.stanford.edu/wp19-06

Riebschleger, J., Day, A., & Damashek, A. (2015). Foster care youth share stories of trauma before, during and after placement: Youth voices for building trauma-informed systems of care. *Journal of Aggression, Maltreatment & Trauma, 24*(4), 339–360. doi:10.1080/10926771.2015.1009603

Roberts, D. E. (1999). Poverty, race, and new directions in child welfare policy. *Washington University Journal of Law and Policy, 1*, 63–76.

Ryan, J. P., Testa, M. F., & Zhai, F. (2008). African American males in foster care and the risk of delinquency: The value of social bonds and permanence. *Child Welfare, 87*(1), 115–129.

Ryan, R., & Deci, E. (2017). *Self-determination theory: Basic psychological needs in motivation, development, and wellness.* Guilford Press.

Shea, N., Zetlin, A., & Weinberg, L. (2010). Improving school stability: An exploratory study of the work of the AB 490 liaisons in California. *Children and Youth Services Review, 32*(1), 74–79. doi:10.1016/j.childyouth.2009.07.013

Smithgall, C., Gladden, R., Howard, E., George, R., & Courtney, M. (2004). *Educational experiences of children in out-of-home care.* Chapin Hall Center for Children at the University of Chicago.

Snyder, T. D. (2018). *Mobile digest of education statistics, 2017* (NCES 2018-138). National Center for Education Statistics, U.S. Department of Education.

Stewart, K., & Thorrington, V., (2019). *Policies and practices to address the educational needs of children in foster care in ten Florida counties.* University of Miami School of Law, Children & Youth Law Clinic. https://issuu.com/miamilaw/docs/policies_and_practices_to_address_t/3

Summers, A. (2015). *Disproportionality rates for children of color in foster care (fiscal year 2013)*. National Council of Juvenile and Family Court Judges. https://www.ncjfcj.org/publications/disproportionality-rates-for-children-of-color-in-foster-care-fiscal-year-2013/

Tucker, V., & Schwartz, I. (2013). Parents' perspectives of collaboration with school professionals: Barriers and facilitators to successful partnerships in planning for students with ASD. *School Mental Health, 5*, 3–14.

U.S. Department of Education. (2019). *The condition of education*. National Center for Education Statistics. https://nces.ed.gov/programs/coe/indicator_cgg.asp

U.S. Department of Health and Human Services. (2020). *Adoption and Foster Care Analysis and Reporting System (AFCARS)* Report No. 27. Administration for Children & Families, Children's Bureau. https://www.acf.hhs.gov/cb/resource/afcars-report-27

Valle, J. W. (2009). *What mothers say about special education: From the 1960s to the present*. Palgrave.

Valle, J. W., & Aponte, E. (2002). IDEA and collaboration: A Bakhtinian perspective on parent and professional discourse. *Journal of Learning Disabilities, 35*(5), 469–479. doi:10.1177/00222194020350050701

Weithorn, L. (2005). Envisioning second-order change in America's responses to troubled and troublesome youth. *Hofstra Law Review, 33*, 1305–1506.

Wilson, B. D. M., Cooper, K., Kastanis, A., & Nezhad, S. (2014). *Sexual & gender minority youth in Los Angeles foster care: Assessing disproportionality and disparities in Los Angeles*. The Williams Institute. https://wwwstage.acf.hhs.gov/sites/default/files/cb/pii_rise_lafys_summary.pdf

Zeitlin, V., & Curcic, S. (2014). Parental voices on Individualized Education Programs: "Oh, IEP meeting tomorrow? Rum tonight!" *Disability & Society, 29*(3), 373–387. doi:10.1080/09687599.2013.776493

Zetlin, A., MacLeod, E., & Kimm, C. (2012). Beginning teacher challenges instructing students who are in foster care. *Remedial and Special Education, 33*, 4–13. doi:10.1177/0741932510362J6

CHAPTER 5

Legislative Blindness

Policy Considerations for Youth Experiencing Homelessness

Deborah Perez

> We are not the sources of problems; we are resources that are needed to solve them. We are not expenses; we are investments. We are not just young people; we are people and citizens of this world. . . . You call us the future, but we are also the present.
>
> —400 Delegates of the United Nations Children's Forum,
> *A World Fit for Us*

LIVING ON THE MARGINS OF SOCIETY: POLICY SUPPORTS FOR YOUTH EXPERIENCING HOMELESSNESS

In cities across the United States, homelessness is a fixture within our communities, and while all experiences of homelessness are troubling, children and youth are considered to be the most vulnerable subset of this population because of the long-term severe effects on childhood and adolescent development (Hart-Shegos, 1999). Research suggests that youth experiencing homelessness are at a higher risk for deleterious life outcomes, including issues with mental health (Hodgson et al., 2013), physical health (Medlow et al., 2014), substance abuse (Greene et al., 1997), violence (Heerde et al., 2014), premature deaths (Auerswald et al., 2016), and early pregnancies (Green & Ringwalt, 1998). Outcomes appear to be even worse for youth who have intersectional identities and have been doubly marginalized due to structural barriers such as racism, sexism, and homophobia (Kulik et al., 2011).

Within an educational context, youth experiencing homelessness face additional challenges, such as absenteeism related to homelessness, issues with transportation, hunger, and poor health, that reduce their abilities to access and attain a quality education, often leading to an increase in school dropout rates. A study conducted by the Center for Promise (2014) revealed that youth who were experiencing homelessness were "87% more likely to stop going to school" (p. 9). We can understand why youth might struggle to perform well in school faced with uncertain shelter and no firm sense of belonging to a community, leading to this alarming statistic.

Shelter and social belonging are basic human needs as articulated in Maslow's (1943) theoretical framing. Maslow's hierarchy of needs postulates that every human being has a basic set of needs that must be met before they can attain their fullest potential. The most basic of these needs are physiological needs, which include shelter, food, security and safety, and a sense of belonging as fundamental prerequisites prior to any human being able to self-actualize. From this perspective, one can assume that without fulfilling the basic need of access to shelter, youth may never achieve their full academic potential.

Youth who experience homelessness are defined by federal law as "individuals who lack a fixed, regular, and adequate nighttime residence" (McKinney-Vento Act, 2009, Section A). Federal data report that at least 1,504,544 youth enrolled in public schools within the United States experienced homelessness in school year 2017–2018 (National Center for Homeless Education, [NCHE], 2018); however, research suggests that this number represents an underreporting of the actual population. Underestimates are likely due to a multitude of reasons, including varying definitions and provisions under law, the clandestine nature of the population, avoidance of the stigma of the homeless label, and the research methods utilized to collect data in depicting the problem accurately (e.g., point-in-time counts; Paterson et al., 2019; Tierney & Hallett, 2011). These reasons provide us with the context to assume that the number of youth who are experiencing homelessness is likely a greater issue than has been delineated and thus demands additional attention.

It is also important to study the structural challenges of homelessness within our systems through the untold stories of those who experience it, and thus uncover the challenges they face in trying to access resources for which the legal provisions do not sufficiently address. Resources and supports for youth experiencing homelessness are outlined by educational policies such as the McKinney-Vento Homeless Assistance Act (MVA; 1987, 2009). While policies are well-intentioned, some youth will fall through the cracks because the legislation does not serve their needs, creating further marginalization among youth experiencing homelessness. In order to advance educational equity for these students, these policies can be critically examined through the use of the intersectionality-based analysis (IBA) lens adapted by Samson and Cavendish (see Introduction, this volume) to identify and understand the structural domains that impact educational inequality.

INTERSECTIONALITY-BASED ANALYTIC FRAME

The IBA framework can allow a more meaningful understanding of the structural inequities that impact youth differently. This framework puts the vulnerable populations being studied at the forefront, identifies the intersectional relationships that impact youth disproportionately, and critically analyzes the systems and policies that reproduce these inequities (Hankivsky et al., 2014). In this chapter, this framework will be used to critically examine and connect the relevant policies on youth supports for those experiencing homelessness. This analysis will demonstrate the need for the inclusion of lived experiences of youth in addition to a critical policy analysis that can add value in providing recommendations and considerations for the reduction of negative experiences of homelessness among youth, and ultimately impact the quality of their education and life outcomes. In addition, IBA explicitly asks researchers to examine their positionality. In this case, what motivates me to do this work, and what values and experiences do I bring to this area of policy or practice?

POSITIONALITY: KNOWLEDGE, VALUES, AND EXPERIENCES

I was 8 years old the first time I experienced homelessness. I vividly recall a FINAL EVICTION NOTICE on our apartment door and all of our belongings thrown outside, on display, for everyone in our community to see. Despite my young age, I recognized in that moment that this was only the beginning to a precarious life that I somehow would have to learn to navigate. While my own experiences with displacement are not representative of all youth experiencing homelessness, this chapter highlights the challenges and promotes an ethic of care for the youth who share a similar story to my own, which is one core reason for my motivation for this research and work.

As a nonprofit professional for over 10 years, my career has primarily focused on the intersections between equity and education, and my early experience has provided me the background to conduct this work. Working with multiple service organizations has given me the experience and honor to be a part of several community initiatives partnering with both youth and adults to end youth homelessness in our community. Additionally, I attended an urban, underserved high school that consistently reported one of the highest proportions of youth experiencing homelessness in the school district. These personal experiences led me to a deeper understanding of the challenges youth experiencing homelessness face, and encouraged me to help and work with other students who were in similar positions.

Also, as a Latina scholar and activist, I have committed to producing work targeting social change for vulnerable populations through policy work that is grounded in the field of special education and community psychology. My core beliefs and values promote the ideals of Community Based Participatory Action Research (CBPAR) and a desire to become a reflective and inclusive practitioner. The IBA framework also asks me to reflect upon what social determinants may affect my perspective as a researcher. As a beneficiary of social services growing up and having lived a childhood of poverty and violence, my personal commitment to helping children and youth thrive has embedded itself in my educational and research pursuits. As such, I focus on critical and humanizing pedagogy in hopes of promoting equity and fostering an integrated approach to research with youth.

HUMANIZING YOUTH EXPERIENCING HOMELESSNESS

As researchers and policymakers, we often quantify the human experience through statistics. While numerical data can be helpful in demonstrating the magnitude of an issue, it can sometimes contribute to psychic numbing and compassion fading (Slovic & Slovic, 2015). Without acknowledging each of these numbers as individual children whose lives are being impacted by the data we collect and the policies we implement, we inadvertently dismiss the "emotion or feeling necessary to motivate action" (Slovic & Västfjäll, 2015, p. 27). Drawing on Bartolomé's (1994/2009) seminal work in humanizing pedagogy, Salazar (2013) eloquently summarizes, "A humanizing pedagogy builds upon the sociocultural realities of students' lives, examines the socio-historical and political dimensions of education, and casts students as critically engaged, active participants in the co-construction of knowledge" (p. 128). Freire (1974/2013) says that to treat children as objects dehumanizes them by "lessening their abilities to act to transform their world" (Au, 2007, p. 180). Therefore, this approach aspires to represent the complexities and multifaceted aspects of youth homelessness and to provide a space where student voice combats the dehumanizing stigmatization of being labeled "homeless." From a humanizing perspective, it is of critical importance that we work in solidarity with youth rather than in isolation from them, which only further marginalizes this already vulnerable population. This humanizing perspective meshes well with utilizing an IBA framework to increase equity among vulnerable populations. To highlight the human experience of homelessness, I share below the words of Asha, a recent college graduate, that describe the fear and anxiety felt when she received a foreclosure notice on her family's home:

> It was a white envelope. I was robbed of my breath by the bolded, crimson letters. After spending the last four years growing academically and using writing as my currency, I never imagined feeling gutted by a set of words. Each successive letter I read increased my doubt, anger,

and despair as I digested the words: "NOTICE OF FORECLOSURE." This home, my grandmother's home, is the only home I've ever known. Raised by my mother and grandmother, I dedicated this safe space to shaping the constructs of my character. From taking my first steps to watching my grandmother's last breath as she lost her battle with cancer, this home allowed me to maintain faith and derive motivation from hopeless situations. Now, this envelope felt like a threat to my identity and deflated my view of achieving upward mobility. Upon being served this notice in January, my mother was working her third job, trying to ensure food was on the table. I wondered what would happen when I told her that despite her efforts to keep our heads above water, the roof over our heads could be taken away.

Before I opened the front door to those four, gentle knocks, I viewed education as the greatest equalizer. However, in spite of being the first in my family to attend college, I was neither equipped nor prepared to respond to the complexities put before me. Out of an inherent sense of responsibility, I wondered how many people in this situation, with no means to draft a legal response, have watched their homes be taken from them. I visualized those who unwillingly remain static in the face of this regrettably common bolded, crimson notice— those who are met with life's challenges staring at them every morning and reason that it's easier to capitulate than fight . . . [however,] silence sets the precedent that living on the margins of society justifies surrendering in the face of systemic adversity.

ONE SIZE DOES NOT FIT ALL:
CONCEPTUALIZING YOUTH HOMELESSNESS

In this section, I use the IBA framework presented by Samson and Cavendish in the Introduction to this volume and respond to the guiding question for education policy and practice regarding how representations of the problem have come about. And how has the framing of the problem changed over time or across different spaces?

Historically, beliefs about the causes of homelessness have fallen into three main typologies that reflect narratives about the construction of poverty: individualistic, pathological, and systemic. In 2010, Gowan termed these typologies "sin-talk," "sick-talk," and "system-talk" (p. 27). "Sin-talk" situates the experiences of homelessness as individualistic, placing the blame on individuals due to their own personal choices that led to their poverty. This ideology has saturated the discourse on homelessness where people have often been treated as having a personal choice in the matter, such as the idea that they have been socially excluded due to their own "unruliness."

"Sick-talk" denotes a medical model of understanding the cause of homelessness as an involuntary response related to mental health and sickness. This was a prominent approach historically and characterizes a century during which many individuals were institutionalized. However, beginning in the 1950s, many asylums began to close, and deinstitutionalization began. This process left many individuals without treatment and without shelter, increasing the need for communities to be responsible for the care of these individuals. This has negatively impacted societal views of mental health issues; we still endure the impact of these views today.

Lastly, "system-talk" refers to understanding homelessness as a "dysfunction of contemporary social and economic policy" (Gowan, 2010, p. 45). This view of homelessness is a focal point of this chapter because it identifies system failures related to homelessness and highlights limited resources for those in need. This typology allows us to explore the structural challenges that influence the implementation and effects of policies. However well-intentioned, these policies impact those experiencing homelessness directly and their relation to that experience must be examined to understand how to improve outcomes for those most affected by it.

These typologies provide a frame for how this problem has been perceived and changed over time and demonstrate the ways in which we must critically examine policies on a consistent basis to prevent and address homelessness and its impacts on our nation's most vulnerable population, our youth. By recognizing the lived experiences and structural challenges that face youth experiencing homelessness, we can begin to analyze how policies can be enhanced to meet the needs of those it intends to serve. Pleace (2000) has emphasized the need for a multidimensional approach to homelessness to account for "the complex interaction of experiences, characteristics and environment" (p. 592). The following section refers to existing policies related to youth experiencing homelessness and how some of these typologies are reflected in the language used.

Utilizing the federal definitions of youth experiencing homelessness provides a guide as to how provisions are currently accessed and distributed to youth via legislation. Established in 1987, the McKinney-Vento Act became the first major federal legislative response to homelessness and remains to this day the only one that provides a range of services to individuals experiencing homelessness, including youth. In addition to the definition that homeless are "individuals who lack a fixed, regular, and adequate nighttime residence" (MVA, 2009, Section A), the following subsections provide additional definitions of youth experiencing homelessness according to various governmental departments, specifying further demarcations of who is considered to be eligible for services. These definitions provide deficit language that reflects Gowan's (2010) typologies and the limiting perspectives that influence the ability of youth experiencing homelessness to access these much-needed supports.

System-Talk

The definition according to the DOE per Title IX, Part A of the Elementary and Secondary Education Act, as amended by the Every Student Succeeds Act (ESSA) in 2015, includes the previous definition, but also extends to include the following (NCHE, n.d.):

> (i) Children and youths who are sharing the housing of other persons due to loss of housing, economic hardship, or a similar reason; are living in motels, hotels, trailer parks, or camping grounds due to the lack of alternative adequate accommodations; are living in emergency or transitional shelters; or are abandoned in hospitals;
>
> (ii) children and youths who have a primary nighttime residence that is a public or private place not designed for or ordinarily used as a regular sleeping accommodation for human beings;
>
> (iii) children and youths who are living in cars, parks, public spaces, abandoned buildings, substandard housing, bus or train stations, or similar settings; and
>
> (iv) migratory children who qualify as homeless . . . because the children are living in circumstances described in clauses (i) through iii).

Unaccompanied youth are also one of the subpopulations considered in the legislation. MVA defines "unaccompanied youth" as follows: "a youth not in the physical custody of a parent or guardian" [42 U.S.C. § 11434a(6)].

Gowan's (2010) "systems-talk" give us the lens in which to review this definition critically. Since systems-talk refers to social and economic policy dysfunctions, it is important to note that the language in this definition including unaccompanied minors reflects a larger systems issue where youth are left unaccompanied due to family economic hardships and to social policies that constrain families from accessing pathways to citizenship so they can legally immigrate with their children to the United States. A policy that addressed immigration and supports for youth and their families would help to mitigate unaccompanied youth experiencing homelessness.

Sick-Talk

To qualify under the definition of "homelessness" according to the Department of Housing and Urban Development (HUD) (2014), an individual must fall under one of the following four categories (slightly modified from HUD information sheet, available at https://files.hudexchange.info/resources/documents/HUDs-Homeless-Definition-as-it-Relates-to-Children-and-Youth.pdf):

1. ***Literally homeless:*** Individuals and families who live in a place not meant for human habitation including in the streets or cars, or in emergency shelters, transitional housing, and hotels paid for by a government or charitable organization.
2. ***Imminent risk of homelessness:*** Individuals or families who will lose their primary nighttime residence within fourteen days and have no other resources or support networks to obtain other permanent housing.
3. ***Homeless under the Federal statutes:*** Unaccompanied youth under 25 years of age, or families with children and youth, who do not otherwise qualify as homeless under this definition, but who: are defined as homeless under the other listed federal statutes, have not had a lease, and/or experienced persistent instability measured by two or more moves in the past 60 days and are likely to remain unstable for an extended period of time due to special needs or barriers.
4. ***Fleeing/attempting to flee domestic violence:*** Individuals or families who are fleeing or attempting to flee domestic violence, dating violence, sexual assault, or stalking, have no other housing, and who lack resources and support networks to obtain other permanent housing.

This definition uses a "sick-talk" approach where conditions for being considered to be homeless are related to issues impacting mental health, yet the policies do not outline supports for addressing some of these traumatic situations that cause youth and their families to experience homelessness in the first place. This definition includes youth at imminent risk for homelessness and fleeing domestic violence, which outlines more of an ameliorative response to these conditions versus a transformative response toward prevention by suggesting that youth must first experience these risky situations prior to receiving supports for homelessness.

Sin-Talk

The Department of Health and Human Services Runaway and Homeless Youth Act of 1974 (RHYA) defines "homeless youth" as individuals who are "less than 21 years of age . . . for whom it is not possible to live in a safe environment with a relative and who have no other safe alternative living arrangement." This definition includes only those youth who are unaccompanied by families or caregivers. This definition applies the sin-talk typology where deficit language in the policy reflects youth as being runaways, which generates a narrative that it was a personal choice that led to these youth experiencing homelessness.

In addition to multiple federal definitions of homeless youth, states and local communities may have their own definitions, creating further difficulty in ascertaining accurate numbers. Issues with identification also impede those experiencing homelessness from accessing appropriate services. Inconsistent definitions across agencies complicate access to resources and supports for youth who have varying experiences of homelessness. "Just as there are no simple explanations for homelessness no uniform experiences of it, there are no easy, one-size-fits-all solutions" (The Night Ministry, 2018). The previous definitions serve an ameliorative response to the experiences of homelessness, where youth are identified after the fact; they do not help to recognize the risks and patterns that lead to experiencing homelessness and thus to determine solutions to prevent it altogether.

Under the reauthorization of MVA in 2015 under ESSA, the definition no longer includes "awaiting foster care placement" (NCHE, n.d.), making it more difficult to provide services to foster care youth, a population vulnerable to homelessness at exacerbated rates (Dworsky et al., 2013). Recognizing the unique experiences of youth in these precarious situations, differential risk factors and acknowledgement of intersectional identities could provide policymakers with insights on how to mediate for youth who are at greatest risk for experiencing homelessness. The IBA framework allows us to critically examine the differential impacts between groups and the inequities that are reproduced through absence of explicit language to meet the nuanced needs of youth experiencing homelessness.

THE DIFFERENTIAL IMPACTS OF HOMELESSNESS

The IBA framework specifically asks researchers to answer the question: Who and what groups are differentially impacted by this issue? Data reveal that subpopulations of those "at-risk" for experiencing homelessness include youth differentially impacted because of their age, gender, sexual orientation, foster care placement, mental health status, and race. However, current federal legislation does not formally recognize these categories of at-risk youth, which can result in "legislative invisibility." Legislative invisibility results when certain classifications of people, like LGBTQ+, are not specifically addressed in a statute; they reap no benefit from it even though it is meant to benefit everyone. This type of invisibility is a consequence of implementing overly generalized policies, which lack nuance, to extend to homeless youth on a national scale. Laws based solely on the experiences of one identity group, when members within the group are also members of varying subgroups, can only provide a limited amount of support (Page, 2017, p. 20).

Thus, ensuring that policymakers attend to subpopulations most disproportionately impacted by youth homelessness may provide a foundation for determining high-impact priority areas.

Age

According to HUD's 2019 point-in-time count data collection for the Annual Homelessness Assessment Report, the large majority (89%) of unaccompanied youth experiencing homelessness were between the ages of 18 and 24, while the remaining 11% were under the age of 18. Thus, many youth experiencing homelessness are older youth who recently exited or dropped out of K–12 systems and likely are not receiving supports provided by the MVA because they are no longer in school and are now "on their own." When youth are not in school, there are several challenges that they face, and their age and developmental stage directly affect their experiences. For example, youth experiencing homelessness are often approached by adults experiencing homelessness and by not being in school, youth are exposed to dangerous interactions with adults that can end in violence, sexual abuse, and drug addiction. To help guard against such outcomes, the MVA could include transition supports for youth aging out of the school system and high school juniors and seniors to better serve youth experiencing homelessness by age group and prevent them from being exposed to conditions that put them even further at risk. As they relate to age, the current policies do not sufficiently address sustainable efforts for youth experiencing homelessness.

Gender

Data generally indicate an even number between male- and female-identified youth experiencing homelessness, though females tend to seek services more often than males (National Coalition for the Homeless, n.d.). However, in 2019, data revealed that 59% of unaccompanied youth experiencing homelessness identified as male (National Coalition for the Homeless, n.d). This trend could be impacted by additional identities that intersect and exacerbate the experience of homelessness such as race, dis/ability, class, and incarceration, where males tend to have higher prevalence rates in each category. These structural barriers doubly marginalize youth and create further inequities (Kulik et al., 2011). Policy should reflect approaches in which services can be universally accessible by all youth, regardless of their gender, and also recognize the importance of intersectional identities that contribute to doubly marginalized youth and prioritize efforts in those areas. In this case, working more closely with youth who identify as males experiencing homelessness, and empowering their voices, could lead to addressing implications for services and eliminating differential impacts by gender.

Sexual Orientation

Several studies highlight the increased risk Lesbian, Gay, Bisexual, Transgender and Questioning (LGBTQ+) youth have in experiencing homelessness (e.g.,

Choi et al., 2015; Durso & Gates, 2012; Morton et al., 2018). Data suggest that LGBTQ+ youth are 120% more likely to experience homelessness compared to youth who identify as heterosexual (Morton et al., 2018). Many of these youth have been disowned by their families and kicked out due to their sexual orientation or identities. Within this population, transgender youth disproportionately experience homelessness. For example, one in five transgender individuals report homelessness due to discrimination and family rejection (National Center for Transgender Equality, n.d.). Pergamit and colleagues (2016) reported that familial connection is considered to be a key protective factor for youth experiencing homelessness, and outlined evidence-based family interventions that support reunification, when possible, which can lead to prevention of homelessness. Federal provisions do not currently outline specific supports for LBGTQ+ youth or their families, and policymakers should consider this subgroup as a primary target for developing programs around improving family relationships to decrease homelessness among LGBTQ+ youth.

Foster Care Placement

Studies have suggested that involvement in foster care may be associated with homelessness, where youth tend to be impacted at an earlier age and for longer durations (Roman & Wolfe, 1997). Correlated to age, at least 22% of youth aging out of foster care (like those aging out of the school system) become homeless within a year (Pecora et al., 2005). This trend suggests that language removed from the MVA regarding youth awaiting placement should be reconsidered in future reauthorizations in order to increase supports for foster care youth in particular, as they tend to be disproportionately impacted by homelessness. In addition, many youth avoid the foster care system altogether due to additional challenges within the system and end up experiencing homelessness as a result. In addition to the differential, deficit language used in legislation around youth experiencing homelessness can be removed to reduce the stigma associated with being in foster care. For example, the Runaway and Homeless Youth Act (1974) defines "homeless youth" as individuals who are "less than 21 years of age . . . for whom it is not possible to live in a safe environment with a relative and who have no other safe alternative living arrangement." This definition applies the sin-talk typology where deficit language in the policy reflects youth as being "runaways," which generates a narrative that it was a personal choice that led to these youth experiencing homelessness.

Mental Health Status

As many as 69% of youth experiencing homelessness indicated having challenges with mental health (Morton et al., 2018). Due to trauma and lack of support, many youth face issues with mental health stability; therefore, policies should include a concrete plan for counseling services for youth in need. While the MVA requests that liaisons provide referral services, many schools lack adequate counselors who could potentially be the first barrier between youth and the deleterious effects that homelessness has on mental health.

Race

A national survey of youth revealed that Black youth are 83% more likely to experience homelessness compared to other races (Morton et al., 2018). Morton et al. posit that disproportionality in homelessness among Black youth emulates racial disparities in other systems such as school discipline, juvenile delinquency, and placements with foster care. They suggest, "It is likely that disproportionalities in other systems, along with a weaker schooling and service infrastructure in predominantly Black communities, help explain elevated risk of homelessness" (p. 13). Thus, policies should consider including strategies that help to monitor and mitigate these inequalities.

INTERSECTIONAL VULNERABILITIES

Factors such as age, gender, sexual orientation, foster care, mental health, and race contribute to youths' vulnerability to experiencing homelessness. For example, a youth experiencing homelessness has lost a fundamental need, which is shelter, but a youth experiencing homelessness who is also in foster care or has been kicked out of their home due to their sexual orientation also suffers impact to another fundamental need, a sense of belonging. Response to multiple social identities can create an exacerbated experience for youth. Many of these factors often intersect, making some multiply vulnerable, especially in navigating the educational terrain. Therefore, further consideration of systemic factors contributing to youth experiencing homelessness should be examined to understand the ways in which society exacerbates these hardships, creating legislative blindness when policies do not specifically name those most impacted by this issue. For example, the MVA addresses specific resources that youth experiencing homelessness need, such as transportation and school supplies, but it does not discuss counseling supports for youth who are in need of professional staff who work with LGBTQ+ youth, or resources to connect these youth with service providers who can help support youth not outlined in the policy. By specifically naming youth whom research shows to be the most at risk for experiencing homelessness, policymakers can outline resources to support these youth.

While the previously discussed typologies, definitions, and statistics express an overarching idea of how homelessness has been conceptualized, viewed, and defined in education legislation, it provides us with merely a snippet of the realities individual youth have faced. Although the MVA provides guidance on the education of youth experiencing homelessness and has been the primary way to address the issue in schools, it has had little effect on the systemic barriers that youth face. Even though policy provisions exist to support youth experiencing homelessness, in implementation, many youth are unable to access these supports because their multiple identities and interrelated issues are not acknowledged by the legislations. Future reauthorizations of the MVA should consider the subgroup populations that are not able to access resources and determine ways in which provisions can reach them.

A major issue of this policy and metaphorical "red tape" restricting access of youth experiencing homelessness is the prerequisite that youth have to disclose their status to a school official. The MVA cannot begin providing services until a student is identified. This criterion presupposes that youth (a) are aware of their rights, (b) are able to navigate the system, (c) feel comfortable and trusting enough to confide in someone to disclose their status, and (d) are willing to admit to the required label of "homeless," which may be something youth are still grappling with. Homeless youth have been said to be "dually stigmatized" (Miles & Okamoto, 2008, p. 428) because of the compounding factors of age, race, and homeless status, which have harsh implications for how these marginalized youth access formal supports in a place that requires them to confront their traumas by labeling themselves.

Hallett and Skrla (2017) underscore that "in the past, schools and districts have primarily focused on helping the students get access to school without considering the support structures needed for the students to more fully access the educational process after registration" (p. 103). The MVA is an example of a policy that does not provide the infrastructure for students to access supports outside of registering for school. The policy should be in alignment with youth experiences and provide youth with access to supports without requiring them to go through extra hurdles to seek these much-needed provisions guaranteed to them by law.

FROM ATOMISTIC TO HOLISTIC APPROACHES

The IBA framework provides a lens for shifting policies, such as the MVA, from atomistic to holistic approaches to resolve immediate issues for youth experiencing homelessness and increase their life chances. Some of the most notable challenges with the current policy are navigating and comprehending of the policy itself for youth experiencing homeless-ness, the need for self-disclosure, and the lack of knowledge of available supports.

I have also highlighted how policies do not consider social markers such as age, gender, sexual orientation, foster care, race, and mental health. Communication and cohesion across community and informal resources could serve to connect youth to accessing resources. Individuals within schools and communities that provide supports to youth in other ways have often already developed a rapport with these youth and could serve as entry points for disclosure and identification. Therefore, training for personnel in schools and communities could allow for better support of these students. The MVA stipulates that professional workshops and trainings will be pro-vided to teachers; however, teachers are often unaware of these opportuni-ties. The inclusion of a state-mandated professional development, similar to child abuse prevention training, for *all* teachers to educate them about vulnerable populations such as youth experiencing homelessness could be a part of policy revision to enhance the knowledge of staff who work on the front lines educating these students, and ultimately improve educational quality for all.

Rothe and Collins (2017) argue that "homelessness is a symptom, not the problem, of the sadomasochistic relationship between the state and its subjects. Without this recognition and rejection of the current integrated spectacle, we remain complicit in the reproduction of inequalities" (p. 15). In order to achieve the goal of preventing and ending homelessness in the United States, we must hold these policies and policymakers accountable by recognizing that there are strengths, assets, and solutions among youth with lived experiences of homelessness. The experience of homelessness is not the problem, but rather policies that may exacerbate outcomes if tangible resources and structural supports are not provided.

CONCLUSION

The MVA policy needs continued revision to include specific strategies for supporting those most impacted by homelessness and to increase awareness of rights and training for youth and other stakeholders across the health, juvenile justice, and child welfare systems so they may adequately respond to the needs of this population of youth. The current policies continue to use deficit language. Through critical examination of the use of sin-talk, sick-talk and systems-talk typologies and the use of an IBA framework, we can identify gaps within policies to enhance the provisions provided to youth experiencing homelessness.

Within the current economic climate, many of us are just one bill away from experiencing homelessness. At the time of writing this chapter, the COVID-19 pandemic is currently affecting and impacting individuals across the globe. The whole world is seeing legislative and institutional actions being enacted overnight to develop policies for public education, health, and legal systems. This contagion has pinpointed some of our country's most severe issues, primarily how quickly employment and housing instability can endanger a person's as well as society's health. Efforts to support youth experiencing homelessness during the pandemic are being made without policy revisions to MVA (e.g., creating access to shelters in communities where housing is being underutilized; creating an infrastructure for food banks at local schools for youth in need), and as such they showcase that unmet needs can easily be addressed if policymakers and local stakeholders understand the issues faced and respond to them in real time and with tangible resources that are accessible by youth.

Unfortunately, it took a worldwide pandemic to jumpstart our nation's actions in supporting policies that create conditions in which youth experiencing homelessness and others can survive. In a world where uncertainty looms, consideration of intersectional vulnerabilities through an IBA lens helps us to recognize where policy development and implementation need revision and can be improved to impact future generations' experiences. Now more than ever, we are presented with an opportunity to reimagine and reinvent the way in which we structure supports for youth experiencing homelessness.

In sum, as we begin to see government and communities coming together to offer resources to those in need, we can see the utility of the IBA framework to analyze policies, as well as of strengths-based approaches for supports. Lastly, by highlighting voices of students who are experiencing these issues, we can begin to envisage new ways to develop innovative systems that diminish their challenges and increase youths' life chances. These implications demand immediate action, as what we do in the present will impact our nation's children and their futures. Youth experiencing homelessness serve as a sober reminder of how society fails to meet children's basic human needs and diminishes the opportunity for them to reach their full potential. Thus, as researchers, policymakers, educators, and ethical human beings, we must acknowledge the need for action to address ways we can eradicate the experiences of homelessness, especially for our nation's most vulnerable children.

REFERENCES

400 Delegates of the United Nations Children's Forum. (2002). *A world fit for us.* United Nations Special Session on Children. https://www.unicef.org/specialsession/press/cfmessage.htm

Au, W. (2007). Epistemology of the oppressed: The dialectics of Paulo Freire's theory of knowledge. *Journal for Critical Education Policy Studies*, 5(2), 175–196. http://www.jceps.com/archives/551

Auerswald, C. L., Lin, J. S., & Parriott, A. (2016). Six-year mortality in a street-recruited cohort of homeless youth in San Francisco, California. *PeerJ*, 4(e1909). https://doi.org/10.7717/peerj.1909

Bartolomé, L. I. (2009). Beyond the methods fetish: Toward a humanizing pedagogy. In A. Darder, M. P. Boltodano, & R. D. Torres (Eds.), *The critical pedagogy reader* (2nd ed., pp. 338–355). Routledge. (Original work published 1994)

Center for Promise. (2014). *Don't call them dropouts: Understanding the experiences of young people who leave high school before graduation*. America's Promise Alliance. https://www.americaspromise.org/sites/default/files/d8/2016 -10/DCTD%20Final%20Full_0.pdf

Choi, S. K., Wilson, B. D. M., Shelton, J., & Gates, G. (2015). *Serving our youth 2015: The needs and experiences of lesbian, gay, bisexual, transgender, and questioning youth experiencing homelessness*. The Williams Institute with True Colors Fund. https://truecolorsunited.org/wp-content/uploads/2015/05/Serving -Our-Youth-June-2015.pdf

Durso, L. E., & Gates, G. J. (2012). *Serving our youth: Findings from a national survey of service providers working with lesbian, gay, bisexual and transgender youth who are homeless or at risk of becoming homeless*. The Williams Institute. https://www.evawintl.org/Library/DocumentLibraryHandler .ashx?id=1164

Dworsky, A., Napolitano, L., & Courtney, M. (2013). Homelessness during the transition from foster care to adulthood. *American Journal of Public Health*, 103(S2), S318–S323. https://doi.org/10.2105/AJPH.2013.301455

Every Student Succeeds Act (ESSA) of 2015, Public Law No. 114–95, S.1177, 114th Cong. (2015). https://www.congress.gov/114/plaws/publ95/PLAW-114publ95 .pdf

Freire, P. (2013). *Education for critical consciousness*. Bloomsbury Academic. (Original work published 1974)

Gowan, T. (2010). *Hobos, hustlers, and backsliders: Homeless in San Francisco*. University of Minnesota Press.

Green, J., & Ringwalt, C. (1998). Pregnancy among three national samples of runaway and homeless youth. *Journal of Adolescent Health*, 23(6), 370–377. https://doi.org/https://doi.org/10.1016/S1054-139X(98)00071-8

Greene, J. M., Ennett, S. T., & Ringwalt, C. L. (1997). Substance use among runaway and homeless youth in three national samples. *American Journal of Public Health*, 87(2), 229–235. https://doi.org/10.2105/ajph.87.2.229

Hallett, R., & Skrla, L. (2017). *Serving students who are homeless: A resource guide for schools, districts, and educational leaders*. Teachers College Press.

Hankivsky, O., Grace, D., Hunting, G., Giesbrecht, M., Fridkin, A., Rudrum, S., Ferlatte, O., & Clark, N. (2014). An intersectionality-based policy analysis framework: Critical reflections on a methodology for advancing equity. *International Journal for Equity in Health*, 13(119), 1–16. https://doi.org/10.1186/ s12939-014-0119-x

Hart-Shegos, E. (1999). *Homelessness and its effects on children*. Family Housing Fund. https://shnny.org/uploads/Homelessness_and_Its_Effects_on_Children.pdf

Heerde, J. A., Hemphill, S. A., & Scholes-Balog, K. E. (2014). 'Fighting' for survival: A systematic review of physically violent behavior perpetrated and experienced by homeless young people. *Aggression and Violent Behavior*, 19(1), 50–66. https://doi.org/10.1016/j.avb.2013.12.002

Hodgson, K. J., Shelton, K. H., van den Bree, M. B. M., & Los, F. J. (2013). Psychopathology in young people experiencing homelessness: A systematic review. *American Journal of Public Health*, 103(6), e24–e37. https://doi.org/10.2105/ajph.2013.301318

Kulik, D. M., Gaetz, S., Crowe, C., & Ford-Jones, E. (Lee). (2011). Homeless youth's overwhelming health burden: A review of the literature. *Pediatrics & Child Health*, 16(6), e43–e47. https://doi.org/10.1093/pch/16.6.e43

Maslow, A. H. (1943). A theory of human motivation. *Psychological Review*, 50(4), 370–396. https://doi.org/10.1037/h0054346

McKinney–Vento Homeless Assistance Act of 1987, P.L. 100-77, 101 Stat. 482, 42 U.S.C. § 11301 et seq. (1987).

McKinney-Vento Homeless Assistance Act, as amended by S.896, The Homeless Emergency Assistance and Rapid Transition to Housing (HEARTH) Act of 2009, P.L. 100-77, 103 Stat. 896, 42 U.S.C. § 11302 et seq. (2009). https://www.hud.gov/sites/documents/HAAA_HEARTH.PDF

Medlow, S., Klineberg, E., & Steinbeck, K. (2014). The health diagnoses of homeless adolescents: A systematic review of the literature. *Journal of Adolescence*, 37(5), 531–542. https://doi.org/10.1016/j.adolescence.2014.04.003

Miles, B., & Okamoto, S. (2008). The social construction of deviant behavior in homeless and runaway youth: Implications for practice. *Child and Adolescent Social Work*, 25, 425–441. https://doi.org/10.1007/s10560-008-0131-3

Morton, M. H., Dworsky, A., Samuels, G. M., & Patel, S. (2018). *Missed opportunities: Youth homelessness in rural America*. University of Chicago.

National Center for Homeless Education. (n.d.). The McKinney-Vento definition of homeless. https://nche.ed.gov/mckinney-vento-definition/

National Center for Homeless Education. (2018). Federal data summary school years 2017–2018: Education for homeless children and youth. https://nche.ed.gov/wp-content/uploads/2020/01/Federal-Data-Summary-SY-15.16-to-17.18-Published-1.30.2020.pdf

National Center for Transgender Equality. (n.d.). *Housing and homelessness*. https://transequality.org/issues/housing-homelessness

National Coalition for the Homeless. (n.d). *Youth homelessness*. http://national-homeless.org/issues/youth/

Night Ministry. (2018, June 18). *The Night Ministry intervenes at the intersectionality of homelessness*. https://www.thenightministry.org/blog/intersectionality-of-homelessness

Page, M. (2017). Forgotten youth: Homeless LGBT youth of color and the runaway and homeless youth act. *Northwestern Journal of Law and Social Policy*, 12(2), 17–45. http://scholarlycommons.law.northwestern.edu/njlsp/vol12/iss2/2

Paterson, S., Perez, D., & Evans, S. (2019). *iCount Miami report*. Engagement, Power, and Social Action Research Team, University of Miami.

Pecora, P., Kessler, R., Williams, J., O'Brien, A. & English, D. (2005). *Improving family foster care: Findings from the Northwest Foster Care Alumni Study*. Casey Family Programs. https://www.casey.org/northwest-alumni-study/

Pergamit, M., Gelatt, J., Runes, C., & Stratford, B. (2016). *Implementing family interventions for youth experiencing or at risk of homelessness*. Urban Institute. https://www.urban.org/sites/default/files/2016/12/05/implementing-family-interventions-for-youth-experiencing-or-at-risk-of-homelessness.pdf

Pleace, N. (2000). The new consensus, the old consensus and the provision of services for people sleeping rough. *Housing Studies, 15*(4), 581–594. https://doi.org/10.1080/02673030050081113

Roman, N. P., & Wolfe, P. B. (1997). The relationship between foster care and homelessness. *Public Welfare, 55*(1), 4–9.

Rothe, D., & Collins, V. (2017). The integrated spectacle: Neoliberalism and the socially dead. *Social Justice, 43*(2), 1–20. https://www.jstor.org/stable/26380300

Runaway and Homeless Youth Act of 1974, Pub. L. 110-378. 42 U.S.C. § 5732 et seq.

Salazar, M. (2013). A humanizing pedagogy: Reinventing the principles and practice of education as a journey toward liberation. *Review of Research in Education, 37*(1), 121–148. https://doi.org/10.3102/0091732X12464032

Slovic, S., & Slovic, P. (Eds.). (2015). *Numbers and nerves: Information, emotion, and meaning in a world of data*. Oregon State University Press.

Slovic, S., & Västjäll, D. (2015). The more who die, the less we care: Psychic numbing and genocide. In S. Slovic & P. Slovic (Eds.), *Numbers and nerves: Information, emotion, and meaning in a world of data* (pp. 27–41). Oregon State University Press.

Tierney, W. G., & Hallett, R. E. (2011). Social capital and homeless youth: Influence of residential instability on college access. *Metropolitan Universities Journal, 22*(3), 46–62. https://journals.iupui.edu/index.php/muj/article/view/20484

U.S. Department of Housing and Urban Development. (2014). *Children and youth and HUD's homeless definition*. Department of Housing and Urban Development. https://files.hudexchange.info/resources/documents/HUDs-Homeless-Definition-as-it-Relates-to-Children-and-Youth.pdf

U.S. Department of Housing and Urban Development. (2019). *Annual Assessment Report (AHAR) to Congress*. Department of Community Planning and Development. https://www.huduser.gov/portal/sites/default/files/pdf/2019-AHAR-Part-1.pdf

Teachers' Responses to Policies Affecting Late-Entering Students With Interrupted Formal Education

Kristin Kibler

In the summer of 2014, the "border kids" were all over the news. Although it was dubbed the "immigration crisis," the United Nations recommended that the United States address it as a refugee crisis and Nazario (2014) rightly stated that we should call it such. I was working as a literacy coach in two urban high schools that received newcomers from Central America when the 2014–2015 school year began. In fact, one of the schools received 117 students from Honduras in the 9th grade alone. Both of these schools were situated in high-poverty neighborhoods and were already strained for resources.

Over the course of that school year, I was able to have some insight into how this unexpected influx played out in the English for Speakers of Other Languages (ESOL) classrooms and the schools at large. Aside from the swelling of class sizes, the range within them was very challenging for the teachers. This was especially true for the content area teachers, who already had a mixture of native speakers of English (NSEs) and students with various ESOL levels. In addition, they were required to prepare their students for state-mandated testing in English. As the ESOL teachers investigated the newcomers' backgrounds, they realized that most, if not all, had gaps in their formal schooling and that they required specialized academic supports. Furthermore, they learned that most of them had entered the United States as unaccompanied minors. It was apparent through the students' stories that many of them had experienced trauma and that they needed supports and services that the teachers and schools were not equipped to provide.

As support personnel, I worked closely with both ESOL and content area teachers as they tried to differentiate instruction and accommodate the needs of all their students. This led me to search for solutions and then to the realization that there was a paucity of research about how to best serve adolescent students with interrupted formal education (SIFE). This experience was the deciding factor in my pursuing a doctoral degree, as well as the inspiration for the research project that is the focus of this chapter.

The intersectionality-based analysis (IBA) frame, presented by Samson and Cavendish in the Introduction to this volume, prompts researchers to reflect upon who we are and what motivates us to do this work, as well as who is being studied and why. It also asks us to examine how interactions at individual levels of experience are linked to social institutions and processes of power. The rest of this chapter summarizes a study I conducted that made use of the IBA frame to understand levels of teacher experience and how they affect the way teachers engage with mandates and policies. I present findings and implications and recommend changes to state and district policies.

PLACEMENT AND ENTRY INTO U.S. SCHOOLS

According to Sánchez (2014), "federal and state-mandated policies affect such things as immigrant students' right to attend public schools, the language instruction they will receive in school, the composition of their family household, and the opportunity to attend college—to name a few" (p. 363). In the case of the unaccompanied minors from Central America, policies also affect placement and enrollment. When unaccompanied minors are apprehended, their custody and care are transferred to the Office of Refugee Resettlement (ORR) while they await their removal hearings. Following the *Flores v. Reno* settlement (1987), the ORR is required to place unaccompanied minors in the "least restrictive" setting possible "without unnecessary delay." Children who cannot be placed with a sponsor must be transferred to a "licensed facility." It is important to note that during the Trump administration, Congress sought to eliminate Flores protections (Kang, 2018). Following the initial influx, Kandel et al. (2015) reported that the majority of children were placed with immediate family members or extended relatives. In response, the U.S. Department of Education (USDOE) released an information sheet stating, "While residing with a sponsor, unaccompanied children, like other children, are required to attend school up to a certain age established under State law. Sponsors must help unaccompanied children to enroll in school immediately following family reunification" (USDOE, 2015, p. 1).

Although the United States has Supreme Court rulings (e.g., *Lau v. Nichols, Plyler v. Doe*) and federal laws that work together to mandate equal opportunities and access to public education regardless of language and/or immigration status, the type of schooling that is available for immigrant children varies widely. For example, some districts offer newcomer programs, which may range in length from a few weeks to an academic year. These programs typically separate the newcomer students from others and use English as a second language (ESL) rather than bilingual instruction (Menken, 2013). In districts without newcomer programs, immigrant students are often placed directly into the grade level that corresponds with their chronological age. Once placed in a school, newcomers may be mainstreamed into English-only classes and receive some services from an ESL teacher, or they may have some sheltered instruction courses intended to support English language development.

A few states define SIFE and track their academic progress (e.g., New York, Minnesota, Oregon), although there is no federal requirement to do so. Other trajectories for late-entering immigrant students include being counseled out of high schools, needing to work and not attending school, or being shut out and unable to enroll (Lukes, 2014).

CONTEXT OF THE STUDY

The schools that participants were drawn from are situated within a large, urban district in the southeastern region of the United States. They were also within a state that had an "English only" amendment to its constitution. The teachers were expected to abide by this even though the district had a high number of students learning English in school, or emergent bilinguals (see García et al., 2008). According to the district's 2016–2017 statistical highlights, out of a K–12 student body of 356,086, 187,858 students spoke Spanish as their home language and 13,156 students were speakers of Haitian Creole. In this same school year, 72,256 students received ESOL services. No data are available on the percentage of immigrant students who are unaccompanied minors.

Importantly, the teacher workforce in this district was almost the complete inverse of the United States as a whole, where around 82% of public school teachers are White (USDOE, 2016). This district's most recent statistical highlights show that Latinx teachers comprise the greatest part of the teaching workforce at 51.9%. This is followed by Black Non-Latinx at 25.4%, and White Non-Latinx at 20.8%.

In this district, immigrant students were placed in a grade level according to their chronological age. The schools followed the district's ESOL program placement policy, which required a home language survey to be administered upon initial enrollment. If any of the responses were affirmative regarding the use of a language other than English at home, the student was referred for an English proficiency assessment. If their scores placed them in ESOL levels I through IV, they were required to receive ESOL services. At the secondary level, the newcomers who were placed in beginning levels (ESOL levels I and II) took a developmental ESOL course. In addition, all students receiving ESOL services took English language arts (ELA) through ESOL rather than a traditional ELA class. Both the developmental course and language arts class were taught as ESL courses and were intended to provide sheltered instruction, but grade-level English materials were expected to be used in the latter. The ESOL students were typically mainstreamed in all their other classes without the support of push-in or pull-out ESL services. Therefore, students in the ESOL program typically received English-language instruction in required courses such as science, mathematics, and social studies.

The English proficiency assessment included a first language (L1) writing sample. This provided useful information for the ESOL teachers, but the L1 writing data were not tracked in the district database. In short, the district and its schools treated all newcomers as a homogenous group, and SIFE were not defined or treated differently from emergent bilinguals who did not have a history of interrupted formal education.

In order to receive a standard high school diploma, students in this district must earn 24 credits, pass a standardized reading and writing assessment (or earn an equivalent passing score on the ACT or SAT tests), and pass various end-of-course (EOC) assessments in math and science. Furthermore, teachers and schools in this district are held accountable for newcomers' reading and writing scores two years after their date of entry into the United States. The two-year exemption window was granted by the USDOE in 2014; other districts in the state receive only a one-year exemption.

Fourteen out of the fifteen teacher participants in this study were drawn from the two high schools I worked in during 2014–2015. According to the district's 2016–2017 statistical highlights, the percentage of students experiencing poverty at those schools ranged from 21.5% to 24.5% higher than the district average. The percentage of students identifying as a race other than White is also higher than average. The fifteenth participant was teaching in the largest GED program in the district. It was housed within a high school as a school-within-a-school model, and served refugee-background students aged 16 and up.

METHODS

As a White, English-speaking female from the culture of power (Delpit, 1988) who was carrying out research in schools where the majority of the staff and students were people of color and many were first- or second-generation immigrants, it was imperative to center the teachers' experiential knowledge (Solórzano & Yosso, 2001) and highlight their voices. It was also critical to ask the teachers about their perceptions of the students' strengths and how they leverage them while teaching in restrictive, English-only contexts. The research questions were as follows:

1. What are the teachers' experiences in serving late-entering SIFE from the northern triangle countries of Central America who entered during or after the 2014 refugee crisis?
2. What challenges have teachers faced in providing services for these students and how have they addressed those challenges?
3. How do teachers build on the students' strengths and languaging practices in the classroom?
4. How can teachers, schools, and districts improve services for late-entering SIFE?

THEORETICAL FRAMEWORK

Latina/Latino Critical Race Theory (LatCrit) provided an appropriate theoretical framework for centering the teachers' experiential knowledge and lens through which to view the study's findings and implications. LatCrit stemmed from the Critical Race Theory (CRT) movement, in which scholars and activists study and attempt to transform the intersections of power, race, and racism (Delgado & Stefancic, 2012).

Scholars of CRT view race as a social construct, but they also have the awareness that race creates very real lived experiences for people of color (Delgado & Stefancic, 2012). Furthermore, they examine the intersectionality of race along with the other categories that can cause people to be marginalized. In the case of LatCrit, "scholars assert that racism, sexism and classism are experienced amidst other layers of subordination based on immigration status, sexuality, culture, language, phenotype, accent and surname" (Yosso, 2005, p. 73).

PARTICIPANTS

Purposeful sampling was utilized for this project. Following Patton (2015), the participants were selected with the study's purpose, research questions, and data in mind. I was hoping for equal representation in each content area, and was overjoyed to recruit three math teachers, three social studies teachers, three science teachers, and three ELA through ESOL teachers. I also recruited one Developmental ESOL teacher, one high school-based GED teacher, and one participant who taught the focal group of students in a mandatory course for first-year students. Their teaching experience ranged from one and a half to 24 years.

As previously mentioned, the demographics of the teachers in this district look very different from the demographics of teachers in the United States as a whole. This was reflected by the teachers who participated in this study. Of the participants, 67% identify as Latinx, 20% as White, and 13%

as Caribbean Black, with parents who immigrated from Jamaica and Haiti. Just over half of the participants are immigrants themselves (first generation) and one third were from the first generation in their families to be born in the United States (second generation). Pseudonyms were used to protect the teachers' anonymity.

DATA SOURCES

Individual interviews (n=15) provided the data for this study, ranging in length from 40 minutes to an hour and a half. I kept a journal in which I wrote reflective memos and field notes before and/or after each interview. Reflective memos are critical in order "to avoid preconceiving your data" (Charmaz, 2014, p. 165). These memos were especially important due to my position as an insider-outsider (Banks & McGee Banks, 2010) with extensive prior knowledge about the schools, the district, and even some of the participants. This was also an important tool for reflecting upon my positionality.

Two group interviews were held after the initial data analysis was completed, one at each of the two high schools that all but one of the participants were drawn from. This information was used as a member check to test credibility (Lincoln & Guba, 1985). The focus group interviews included member-checking the tentative findings from the analysis of the individual interview data.

DATA ANALYSIS

Grounded theory methods are useful for making inquiries in areas where there has been little prior research (Engward, 2013), which was certainly the case with this topic. In addition, "The premise of grounded theory is that empirical inquiry should explore social phenomena by looking at what people experience, what problems are present and how individuals go about resolving these issues" (Engward, 2013, p. 37). Therefore, grounded theory methods (following Charmaz, 2014) fit well with the purpose of this project. After the interviews were transcribed, I created initial codes to represent chunks of meaning. The next step involved merging these initial codes to create focused codes. Through constant comparison of these initial codes, they were refined into what Charmaz (2014) refers to as "focused codes." After this step, I moved up to the next analytical level by grouping the focused codes that belong together into families (n=25). Again, I followed Charmaz's (2014) approach and stayed close to the patterns that I defined in the data and treated as conceptual categories. The next level of analysis involved exploring the relationships across and between families in order to generate themes (n=6).

These families and themes were member-checked in focus group interviews with the participants (n=2) before moving up to the highest analytical level.

Instead of producing a substantive theory, this research project produced a theoretical statement. The theoretical statement sits at the top of the analytic pyramid and is grounded in the themes themselves. This statement is not transferable, but captures the experiences and perceptions of the participating teachers of late-entering Central American SIFE refugees in their specific contexts.

FINDINGS AND IMPLICATIONS

The IBA frame asks us to consider who the research is for and how it advances the perspective of those under study. In alignment with that as well as the theoretical framework, the following section aims to highlight the participants' voices.

Theoretical Statement

The theoretical statement was crafted to capture the themes that emerged in the analysis: Although teaching late-entering refugees from Central America presents particular educational challenges that the teachers perceive to be exacerbated by the students' unaddressed trauma and needs; structural and political barriers that they face; difficulties they have in adjusting to cultural, educational, and economic circumstances; and pressures from standardized testing, the teachers responded by creating a safe and productive learning environment, leveraging the students' multiple strengths in the classroom, and going above and beyond what their position requires.

Ruptures in the Graduation Pipeline

According to Solórzano (2009), there are "enormous leaks" in the high school graduation pipeline for some Latinx students, and the numbers are even worse when looking at noncitizens (p. xii). Although there are many reasons for the leaks and ruptures, the causes that emerged in both the literature review and the study's findings will be discussed below.

Pipeline leaks from graduation requirements, testing, and standardized curricula. The literature clearly demonstrates that stringent graduation requirements and high-stakes testing are detrimental for late-entering SIFE and those who serve them. The present study supports these findings, but also extends them in showing additional challenges presented to teachers and students due to the inaccessibility of the mandated, assessment-aligned, standardized curricula. The pacing guides that content area teachers must follow and the curricula they are expected to use are aligned with the content standards that the students will be tested on. Some content area teachers do receive some supplementary materials for newcomers, but this is insufficient. The grade-level English curricula are not only inaccessible, but they are not relevant to the students' lives. The teachers have to go to great lengths to create and locate materials and to plan lessons that are relevant.

Leaks stemming from under-resourced, unsupportive, subtractive schools. The literature shows that immigrant students typically attend segregated, under-resourced schools, as was the case for the sites in this study. These schools were situated in a county-wide district and one could argue that funding is distributed equally, but not equitably. In order to receive equitable distributions, the schools serving these students would need additional funding, resources, training opportunities, and personnel.

My findings that the Central American newcomers experienced trauma pre-flight, during flight, and upon resettlement are strongly supported in the literature about refugee-background youths. However, the teachers in this study reported that these traumas go unaddressed. They overwhelmingly talked about the need for social workers, counselors, funded programs, and additional support staff. Furthermore, the teachers talked about several of the students having unmet basic needs (e.g., food scarcity, unstable housing, and homelessness) and legal needs, and needing to work to support themselves or their families. In addition, all of the novice teachers discussed their need for targeted professional development and support to effectively serve late-entering newcomers, and the veteran teachers discussed their need for time and support to reach out to parents and guardians and provide them with information.

The literature demonstrates that schools can be unwelcoming for late-entering newcomers/refugees, and the findings indicate that this was true for the study sites. Although the teachers did not use the word "subtractive" while describing how the larger school climate denied students' cultural backgrounds and enforced assimilationist methods, the focus group participants unanimously agreed when I shared what the term meant (see Valenzuela, 1999). Teachers at each site talked about the ESOL students being isolated and stigmatized, and stated that this was particularly true for the SIFE who were not taught the norms of U.S. schools. They shared stories of other teachers and staff not knowing about or understanding their experiences, and holding deficit perspectives of the students and their abilities. Finally, they provided examples of the schools not being welcoming sites for students and parents. This included the lack of parental outreach, the lack of Spanish-speaking office staff and counselors, and important information being relayed only in English.

The literature points to some typical challenges that arise in serving late-entering refugee-background students, such as the students being placed in teachers' classes with little information or notice and being placed in classes with NSEs. The teachers in this study also noted these challenges, but added to them in talking about the difficulty of newcomers being placed in their classes throughout the school year and the unfairness of the students' end-of-course assessment scores affecting their performance ratings. Furthermore, the variation within beginning ESOL levels emerged as a challenge in this study where it did not in the literature review. The teachers overwhelmingly stated that there is wide variation across ESOL level 1 students depending on the individual student's educational history. This range made planning and delivery difficult, especially in mixed-level/language classrooms. Furthermore, it was up to the teachers to investigate their students' levels and backgrounds. The district did not track this information, although it would be beneficial in serving the students.

Teachers' Responses to Rupture-Sustaining Policies and Practices

Although the overall school climates were subtractive, all the teachers strove to establish and maintain a safe and productive learning environment and build upon the students' strengths. While highlighting the importance of this, Isabella stated, "They have to feel that sense of safety first. You can't really be concerned with learning unless your well-being and your needs are taken care of first." To achieve this, the teachers did what they could to help the students within and outside of their classroom walls.

Creating a safe and productive learning environment. The importance of creating a safe, positive, and productive learning environment came through clearly. The teachers emphasized the importance of making their classrooms welcoming and establishing relationships with their students. Several teachers spoke about this in terms of forming a community and remarked that the students were very good at building this. They also stated that it was highly beneficial for teachers to speak Spanish and understand the students' cultures.

A critical part of the teachers' relationship-building process was showing the students that they cared. In the words of Violeta, "I think what they need is a bit of TLC, tender loving care, 'cause they don't have that anymore. And someone who listens to them." Several teachers talked about how the focal students needed and responded well to caring teachers. A few ways that they demonstrated caring was through talking to the students, teaching the norms and etiquette of high school, being role models and providing guidance, providing constant encouragement, and having high expectations for their work.

Instructional strategies. The teachers listed multiple instructional and grouping strategies that they use to ensure a productive learning environment.

Notably, they were not supposed to use several of these strategies due to the state's English-only policy.

The importance of limiting teacher talk and making the classroom student-centered came through clearly. To accomplish this, the teachers talked about individualizing lessons to meet the students' needs, doing a lot of partner and group activities, and providing scaffolding. For the latter, the teachers attempted to make the content accessible through the use of videos and other visual aids (e.g., timelines, photos, posters, foldables, graphic organizers), simplified language, translation, bilingual instruction, relatable lessons, extended time, and teacher and peer support.

All the teachers also allowed for translanguaging in their classrooms. According to García (2009), "translanguagings are multiple discursive practices in which bilinguals engage in order to make sense of their bilingual worlds" (p. 45). For example, the teachers allowed the use of the students' L1 for clarification and discussions, for demonstrating comprehension, and for prewriting and brainstorming activities. They also used various strategies to encourage the focal students to feel comfortable speaking aloud, and noted that this was especially needed in classrooms where they are mixed with NSEs.

Teachers going above and beyond. It was evident that the teachers were working very hard and doing what they could within their classrooms, and also outside them. At one of the schools, the ESOL teachers and some content area teachers meet regularly to discuss the students and talk about how they could better support them. Many of the teachers offered tutoring after school. Violeta and Santiago were also volunteering as soccer coaches and encouraging their students to play. The majority of them were trying to bridge the gap created by the lack of counseling and social work services. A few examples include explaining required courses and credits, translating for site-based counselors, and trying to connect their students with outside resources. María and Olivia had knowledge of the U.S. legal system and assisted with their students' asylum cases. Olivia called the students' lawyers, negotiated their fees, and offered free translation services. Zoe was networking in order to start a newcomer club. All the novice teachers were seeking additional training and support to be more effective. These efforts required time outside of the school day. María, the ESOL teacher who stayed at least three additional hours after school every day, said, "I love my career. Most of the time I spend hours and hours. I love to learn too."

RECOMMENDATIONS

In their research-based report on making education more equitable for emergent bilingual students, García et al. (2008) make the case for the following: Providing late-exit bilingual/dual language programs tailored to meet linguistic and academic needs; utilizing fair and valid assessments that untangle academic English proficiency from content knowledge; providing quality instruction, adequate resources, and equal opportunities; and involving families and communities in education. States and districts collectively have the power to make each of those things happen.

State-Level Recommendations

States should revise and resubmit their ESSA plan, and they can include SIFE. Minnesota provides an example of this, as they implemented a statewide definition and included students with interrupted formal schooling in their plan. New Mexico is an interesting state to watch following the results of the *Yazzie/Martinez v. State of New Mexico* decision in 2014 and the 2018 gubernatorial election. A judge ruled that the state was not providing the education that its constitution mandates to emergent bilinguals, students receiving special education services, students from lower-socioeconomic-status households, and Native American students. The newly elected governor ran on that issue and ensured that the state would not challenge the lawsuit, but rather, would enact the required policies. The lieutenant governor holds a PhD in education, and the state's new leaders have set up a transformation team with over 100 years of collective educational experience. New Mexico's revised ESSA plan includes ending the use of the Partnership for Assessment of Readiness for College and Careers (PARCC) standardized tests and disbanding their high-stakes accountability system for teachers, students, and schools. New Mexico's revised ESSA plan also provides a model for providing districts with more power, flexibility, and funding. Interestingly, Louisiana offers an example of a conservative state that was able to support the expansion of dual language programs via its ESSA plan.

States also hold the power to authorize in-state tuition for undocumented college students, and at the time of writing, 18 have done so. Once again, New Mexico provides a model, since the state not only offers in-state tuition for undocumented college students, but also provides grants since they are ineligible for federal financial aid (Perez, 2009).

District-Level Recommendations

The findings of both the literature review and the present study demonstrate the need for flexible pathways and extended learning opportunities in order for late-entering SIFE to obtain a standard diploma. In addition, the findings indicate that late-entering newcomers need support transitioning in and out of high school. Districts can implement newcomer and postsecondary transition programs to assist with these processes.

In an email thread with Brenda Custodio (personal communication, May 24, 2019), a renowned expert on newcomer programs, I was told that the Fort Worth Independent School District (FWISD) runs an exemplary 1-year program called the International Newcomer Academy. Custodio also stated that some of the programs of the Internationals Network headquartered in New York City provide good models. Districts should look at effective programs such as these, and implement models that would work well for their newcomers. The literature also suggests that bridge programs that help students transition from newcomer programs into traditional high schools are effective.

Districts should provide additional funding, resources, personnel (e.g., bilingual teachers, social workers, counselors, paraprofessionals), and professional learning opportunities to schools serving late-entering SIFE and/or refugee-background students. The literature talks about the need for ongoing professional development and support, particularly for integrating language into course content, curriculum development, teaching SIFE, refugees, and/or undocumented students, and using asset and critical pedagogies. It is also beneficial for teachers to learn about the experiences of asylum-seekers and refugees, and about the structural barriers that they face, in order to counter deficit perspectives. The literature suggests that teachers should be given the autonomy to develop relevant and accessible curriculum and assessments.

Finally, the literature demonstrates that district support can, and should, extend into the surrounding community. School districts should allow teachers, counselors, and social workers the much-needed time for parental and community engagement. Importantly, districts should form agreements between their schools and programs or organizations to help students and families meet basic, medical, psychological, and legal needs. There are nonprofit organizations that partner with schools to provide additional social workers and supportive programming.

CONCLUSION

James Banks (1998) stated that "the educational policies supported by mainstream social science and educational researchers have often harmed low-income students of color" (p. 5). Since my insider knowledge of the language and culture of power in the United States is a potential blind spot, I try to always be aware of my positionality and how I can use my power to help and not cause further harm. Consideration of the IBA framework questions was beneficial to this end. In fact, the first question forced me to consider my motivations and positionality. IBA asks us to consider if the aims of the research project reflect self-identified needs or needs identified by the affected groups or communities, and if the project is contextualized.

In response, I try to honor my participants' pleas to "do something" with the study's findings. As the IBA frame asks researchers to think about who the research is for and how it advances the perspectives of those under study, it affirms this pursuit and reminds me that my responsibilities to my participants do not end once the study is complete. I also considered this question as I presented implications and recommendations by ensuring that these sections were well-aligned with the study's findings as well as the academic literature.

Finally, the IBA framework asks us to consider which issues of domination/exploitation and resistance/agency are addressed by the research. This aligns well with critical theoretical frameworks such as CRT and LatCrit. Relatedly, the IBA framework challenges us to consider how commonalities and differences will be recognized without resorting to essentialism, false universalism, or obliviousness to historical patterns of inequality. This is critical in carrying out research that recognizes issues and differences without reproducing deficit-laden narratives and inequities, and thus carrying out research that causes further harm.

REFERENCES

Banks, J. A. (1998). The lives and values of researchers: Implications for educating citizens in a multicultural society. *Educational Researcher, 27*(7), 4–17.

Banks, J. A., & McGee Banks, C. A. (2010). Multicultural education: Characteristics and goals. In J.A. Banks & C.A. McGee Banks (Eds.), *Multicultural education issues and perspectives* (7th ed., pp. 3–30). John Wiley & Sons.

Charmaz, K. (2014). *Constructing grounded theory* (2nd ed.). Sage.

Delgado, R., & Stefancic, J. (2012). *Critical race theory: An introduction.* New York University Press.

Delpit, L. D. (1988). The silenced dialogue: Power and pedagogy in educating other people's children. *Harvard Educational Review, 53*(3), 280–298.

Engward, H. (2013). Understanding grounded theory. *Nursing Standard, 28*(7), 37–41.

García, O. (2009). *Bilingual education in the 21st century: A global perspective.* Wiley-Blackwell.

García, O., Kleifgen, J. A., & Falchi, L. (2008). *From English language learners to emergent bilinguals* (Equity matters: Research review No. 1). Teachers College, Columbia University.

Kandel, W. A., Bruno, A., Meyer, P. J., Seelke, C. R., Taft-Morales, M., & Wasem, R. E. (2015). Unaccompanied alien children: Potential factors contributing to recent immigration. *Current Politics and Economics of the United States, Canada, and Mexico, 17*(3), 453–483.

Kang, S. (2018, September 14). Trump's new attack on immigrant children. *ACLU immigrants' rights project.* https://www.aclu.org/blog/immigrants-rights /immigrants-rights-and-detention/trumps-new-attack-immigrant-children

Lincoln, Y. S., & Guba, E. G. (1985). *Naturalistic inquiry.* Sage.

Lukes, M. (2014). Pushouts, shutouts, and holdouts: Educational experiences of Latino American young adults in New York City. *Urban Education, 49*(7), 806–834. doi:10.1177/0042085913496796

Menken, K. (2013). Emergent bilingual students in secondary school: Along the academic language and literacy continuum. *Language Teaching, 46*(4), 438–476. doi:10.1017/S0261444813000281

Nazario, S. (2014, July 11). The children of the drug wars: A refugee crisis, not an immigration crisis. *The New York Times*. https://www.nytimes.com/2014/07/13 /opinion/sunday/a-refugee-crisis-not-an-immigration-crisis.html

Patton, M. Q. (2015). *Qualitative research & evaluation methods: Integrating theory and practice* (4th ed.). Sage.

Perez, W. (2009). *We are Americans: Undocumented students pursuing the American dream*. Stylus Publishing.

Sánchez, P. (2014). Dignifying every day: Policies and practices that impact immigrant students. *Language Arts, 91*(5), 363–371.

Solórzano, D. G. (2009). Foreword. In W. Perez, *We are Americans* (pp. xi–xv). Stylus Publishing.

Solórzano, D. G., & Yosso, T. J. (2001). Critical race and LatCrit theory and method: Counter story telling. *International Journal of Qualitative Studies in Education, 14*(4), 471–495.

United States Department of Education. (2015). *Information on the rights of unaccompanied children to enroll in school and participate meaningfully and equally in educational programs*. https://www2.ed.gov/about/overview/focus /rights-unaccompanied-children-enroll-school.pdf

United States Department of Education. (2016). *The state of racial diversity in the educator workforce*. https://www2.ed.gov/rschstat/eval/highered/racial-diversity /state-racial-diversity-workforce.pdf

Valenzuela, A. (1999). *Subtractive schooling: U.S.-Mexican youth and the politics of caring*. State University of New York Press.

Yosso, T. J. (2005). Whose culture has capital? A critical race theory discussion of community cultural wealth. *Race Ethnicity and Education, 8*(1), 69–91. doi:10.10/1361332052000341006

APPLICATION OF INTERSECTIONALITY-BASED ANALYSIS IN RESEARCH

CHAPTER 7

Advancing the Educational Equity Agenda

Identity Responsiveness as an Approach to Recruiting and Retaining Black Male Special Educators

Patrice Fenton

The equity agenda in education requires us to examine the systemic barriers that preclude all children from getting the education they deserve. It also requires us to reckon with the fact that these barriers exist by design; that is, the system is not at all "broken." To the contrary, it is doing exactly what it was designed to do: create access for some, while others slip through cracks that often lead to deepened fissures of economic disadvantage (Hopson & Lee, 2011). Moreover, these lines of economic dis/advantage exist by categories of identity, which then become weaponized to perpetuate inequity. And through these layered and interconnected categories of identity, a double, and sometimes triple or quadruple, jeopardy is born. For example, a Latinx male student with a learning disability is likely exposed to an inequitable education experience at the intersection of his ethnicity, gender, language, and ability (Brobbey, 2018). Research has also shown that a Black student with a disability is 3.6 times more likely than their White peers with a disability to be suspended from school (Sullivan et al., 2014).

On the teacher side of the equation, for example, a Black male teacher, by virtue of his race and gender, is often relegated to serving as the go-to disciplinarian in schools (Brockenbrough, 2015). This essentializing notion of a Black man's positionality and role in a school links to the idea that these men should be charged with solving the "black boy problem" (Rezai-Rashti & Martino, 2010). While there is no doubt that racial and gender congruence can have great impact on students of color (Gershenson et al., 2017), projecting this role onto Black men places their teacher identities in a proverbial box and inhibits their ability to fully actualize their pedagogical acumen.

In this light, without full recognition of inequity's deep connection to the multitude of identities we assume, we are likely to fall short in our quest for equity. Consequently, as we craft policies, practices and research to tackle issues that are both layered and linked to the very essence of how we identify ourselves, intersectionality as an analytic frame becomes a useful tool to disrupt inequities in our schools. This chapter elucidates how intersectionality can be employed when conducting research, and more specifically, in inquiry around teacher diversity efforts.

TEACHER DIVERSITY AND ITS ROOT CAUSE

Acknowledging the ethnoracial incongruence between our predominantly White and female teaching force and mostly minoritized student population (Albert Shanker Institute, 2005; Bristol & Martin-Fernandez, 2019) has been a great first step in teacher diversity efforts. Studies have shown that teacher diversity and racial congruence between teachers and students can improve achievement outcomes for youth in public schools (Banerjee, 2018). For example, a study showed that a Black boy receiving instruction from a Black teacher in grades 3 through 5 reduces that student's risk for high school dropout (Gershenson et al., 2017). This is particularly true for Black boys from economically disadvantaged backgrounds. We see a similar phenomenon hold true when it comes to leaders of color serving at the helm of our schools. For example, a study has shown that Black students are less likely to be suspended when attending a school led by a person of color (Kress, 2019).

These studies demonstrate that we recognize identity markers as a key component of how inequity persists. However, making efforts to change the "color" of our teaching workforce to improve student outcomes is only the tip of the iceberg. This sort of focus runs the risk of situating the issue in the people who comprise the system (i.e., teachers and students), without taking into account the pitfalls of the system itself (i.e., racist policies and practices) (Rezai-Rashti & Martino, 2010). To this end, we not only need an ecological consideration of the preconditions that perpetuate the lack of diversity in the first place (i.e., situate a racist system as the root cause), but we also need to focus on creating the identity-centered mechanisms that support the recruitment and retention of marginalized groups who enter the teaching profession if we ever plan to realistically fulfill diversity aims.

INTERSECTIONALITY AS A FRAME

Considering that the root cause of teacher diversity issues can be linked to the systemic oppression of people of color and White male patriarchy (Brockenbrough, 2012), intersectionality, with its roots in feminist epistemology (Collins, 1991; Crenshaw, 1991), is a fitting tool and foundation upon which to tackle this persistent concern. Intersectionality recognizes how social inequality manifests through multiple lines of identity that impact one another. As Collins and Bilge (2016) state:

> When it comes to social inequality, people's lives and the organization of power in a given society are better understood as being shaped not by a single axis of social division, be it race or gender or class, but by many axes that work together and influence each other. (p. 2)

As Carbado (2013) indicated, intersectionality is not solely meant to address the sort of double jeopardy referred to above, though it does so in part. What it does is critically acknowledge the complex interwoven manner in which identities (race, class, gender, sexuality, ethnicity, nation, ability, age, etc.) are used to shape inequality (Collins, 2015). Consequently, in this manner, the binary thinking that is at the foundation of Eurocentric patriarchal thought and therefore the foundation of our country's racist systems and practices is rejected (Collins, 1991). This is a necessary part of the root cause analysis; as Collins goes on to note, "The emphasis on quantification and categorization occurs in conjunction with the belief that either/or categories must be ranked. The search for certainty of this sort requires that one side of a dichotomy be privileged while the other is denigrated" (p. 225).

In this light, using an intersectionality-based analysis (IBA) frame for research proves itself appropriate to combat the lack of teacher diversity in our schools. Not only is no one identity valued over another, the interconnectedness of all identities is included in an IBA frame, which therefore can help ensure that it remains considered as policies and practices are put in place. In research, as demonstrated below, identity is not an afterthought. Rather, IBA places who we are at the center of the work, for both researcher and the researched. This humanizes inquiry and, in the instance of teacher diversity, takes us away from solely focusing on the quantitative aspects of teacher diversity (i.e., how many of each racial group comprise the teaching population). Instead, it turns our focus toward how these groups experience the teaching act through the lens of their self-identified, socially contextualized realities.

INVESTIGATING THE CALL FOR MORE BLACK MALE TEACHERS OF COLOR

The lack of teacher diversity spurred the field to make a call for more Black men to enter the teaching force (Lewis & Toldson, 2013). While this is a necessary and worthy call, many layered questions arise when one goes beyond just looking at individual characteristics and examines the ecological factors that surround the aspiration for increased Black male representation in the profession (Bronfrenbrenner, 1977). This would include an assessment of the various systems that individuals are embedded in and affected by (e.g., school, district, societal). For example, is it enough to augment recruitment efforts for this marginalized group, or do we also need to consider its members' sociohistorical experiences in this country as we do so? Additionally, what kinds of barriers to entry exist for this group (Eubanks & Weaver, 1999)? Moreover, what type of supports might they need once they enter the profession? How much are the Black men who are already in the profession truly valued and supported in doing their work effectively? Furthermore, is the call for more Black men to enter the profession a faulty panacea for issues in education that are really systemic and therefore extend deeper than just improving teacher diversity?

The purpose of this study, further explicated below, was to explore some of these questions that arise as one considers the call for more Black men in the teaching profession, particularly as these questions relate to their racial and gendered identities. In the special education context, on which this study was centered, these questions become even more suggestive. This is particularly the case because researchers have found that Black boys have the highest risk of receiving special education labels for high-incidence disabilities (i.e., learning disabilities) (Sullivan & Bal, 2013). It is therefore important to consider the academic trajectories of the Black men we are asking to return to classrooms and school buildings, spaces that may have not been safe spaces for them to begin with.

Consequently, the aims of this study were as follows:

- To honor the voices of Black male special educators and examine their racialized and gendered identities as a way of understanding how they make meaning of their schooling and teaching experiences.
- To recognize Black male special educators as a source of pedagogical knowledge and expertise
- To seek to understand Black male special educators' experiences as a means for improving not only how we serve special education students in urban settings, but also how we prepare the special educators who serve them

In light of these aims, this study sought to answer the following research questions:

Meta-question: What roles do race and gender play in the pedagogies of Black male special educators?
  » Sub-question 1: What roles do race and gender play in the identity construction of Black male special educators?
  » Sub-question 2: What roles did Black men's race and gender play in their decision to become teachers and, more specifically, special educators?

» Sub-question 3: How are Black male special educators going about realizing the aims that drove them to become special educators?

» Sub-question 4: In what ways have Black male special educators been able to realize the aims they set for themselves within their pedagogical practice?

INTERSECTIONALITY AS A CONCEPTUAL FRAMEWORK

The power of using intersectionality as a conceptual framework in the study was founded in its allowance of an ecological lens and the ability for research participants to identify themselves in varied ways. This then allowed for within-group differences to surface in the ways individuals made meaning of their experiences (Garcia & Ortiz, 2013). As the research questions above were crafted, intersectionality pushed for the links between the individual, the teaching act (which includes students, colleagues, and parents), community, the larger society, power structures, and systemic factors (Collins, 2015; Garcia & Ortiz, 2013) to take the fore. In this light, the framework helped probe how individuals self-identify and the categories society places them in, as well as the power and authority those categories have in shaping their realities (Artiles, 2013).

The complexities that intersectionality owns in its assumptions came to bear as this study touched upon the duality of the participants functioning as men who are also a racialized other within a society where (White) male privilege is a norm, *and* in a profession where colleagues are predominantly White and female (Brockenbrough, 2012; Lynn & Jennings, 2009). Yet, while this study's primary intent was not to appraise patriarchal and masculinist forms of thought and how they played out in the work of Black male special educators, there was space for this to come out during data collection or analysis, if need be.

Lastly, as stated by Harry (1996), "In qualitative research, the researcher is seen as the research 'instrument'" (p. 292). As such, intersectionality also created space for me to situate my own positionality within the research as a former public school special educator and marginalized woman of color. This allowed me to firmly claim my status as an outsider-within (Collins, 1991). Further, it created a certain informed subjectivity (Harry, 1996) and reflexivity in the research (Guba & Lincoln, 2005) that also acknowledged the interpersonal dynamics embedded in the relationship between researcher and participant (Garcia & Ortiz, 2013). More specifically, as a Black woman who has had the honor of working alongside more Black male educators than is typical in the field, I have seen firsthand the critical importance of their work and the need to include their voices. In this way, I sought to contribute to disrupting the prevalence and persistence of deficit views of Black men. To this end, it was important that I employ research methods that both complemented the IBA frame and supported my personal connection to the work.

METHODOLOGY

In an attempt to stay true to the layered nature of intersectionality as a conceptual framework, this study employed a methodological approach that was definitive, yet fluid, and allowed for the complexities of the framework to come through in data collection and analysis. The aim was to ensure that the contexts under investigation were as closely connected to the reflected patterns (Engward, 2013) of the researcher's and participants' shared meaning-making (Charmaz, 2006; Denzin & Lincoln, 2005) as possible. Furthermore, as the pursuit of some objective reality was not central to this research, maintaining this layered lens contributed to the decision to employ qualitative research methods.

Using grounded theory methodology with a constructivist lens inherently called for the use of multiple methods (Charmaz, 2006; Denzin & Lincoln, 2005). Consequently, the research also employed elements of narrative inquiry. Grounded theory allowed for the generation of "a theory, an abstract analytical schema of a phenomenon, that relates to a particular situation. This situation is one in which individuals interact, take actions, or engage in a process in response to phenomena" (Cresswell, 1998, p. 56). As such, utilizing two approaches cultivated openness toward whatever the research site revealed, bringing a focused flexibility that allowed for a wide scope without losing hold of the nuanced details that emerged (Charmaz, 2006).

With a focus on the biographies of Black men and their practical experiences in the teaching profession, the research design invoked the African American oral tradition (Banks-Wallace, 2002) through narrative inquiry concepts (Cresswell, 1998; Xu & Connelly, 2010). Utilizing an intersectionality-based approach as a frame to consider how my own identity shaped the research design led me to center these factors. As a result, the shared experience of serving as a minoritized public school special educator between myself as the researcher and participants was one that facilitated the research.

In light of this shared experience, narrative inquiry became a crucial component that connected to identity and fruitful data collection, as the act of storytelling creates a connection between the teller and the listener (Banks-Wallace, 2002). It is through this connection that I sought to honor the voices of Black male special educators and provide a vehicle for them to augment the discourse in the field around teacher diversity efforts. Moreover, it has been argued that the act of storytelling has not only shaped the African American experience in this country, but Gates also suggested that there is great power in using stories to answer epistemological questions, as they have played a pivotal role in the survival of African Americans (as cited in Banks-Wallace, 2002, p. 412).

This survival of African Americans and the essence of the African American oral tradition is founded in an African worldview that, in part, gives great credence to the spoken word (Alkebulan, 2013). As Hamlet (2011) stated, "The Africans believed in Nommo, which means the generative power of the spoken word. Nommo was believed necessary to actualize life and give man mastery over things" (p. 27). This power of the spoken word linked to the research aim of giving voice to the marginalized and oft silenced. Methodologically, as it pertains to voice, Guba and Lincoln (2005) stated the following, "Today voice can mean, especially in more participatory forms of research, not only having a real researcher—and a researcher's voice—in the text, but also letting research participants speak for themselves" (p. 209). As such, this lens informed my line of questioning and helped me adhere to the tenets of intersectionality as an analytical frame.

The study took place in a large urban school district. Using purposive sampling (Merriam, 2009; Patton, 2002), six Black male certified special educators working in secondary public schools were recruited for this study. Table 7.1 below outlines the profile of teachers who were engaged in this study.

Table 7.1. Participant Information

Name	Years Teaching	Borough Taught	Grade(s)	Special Education Setting	Content Area
Calvin	6	Manhattan	High School	ICT, SETSS	English
Francis	6	Brooklyn	Middle School	ICT	History, Math
Kwame	6	Brooklyn	7th	ICT	Science
Rashid	6	Brooklyn	High School	Self-Contained	History
Stephen	3	Bronx	Middle School	ICT, Self-Contained	Literacy, Technology
Vincent	12	Brooklyn	8th	ICT	Math

Note: Integrated Co-Teaching (ICT): a classroom setting with one general educator and one special educator. Special Education Teacher Support Services (SETSS): a special educator works with special education students in a small group in the general education setting or in a separate location.

As a means of meeting the goal of giving voice to Black male special educators while remaining rooted in narrative thinking and African-American oral traditions, each participant experienced two 90-minute individual interviews (Seidman, 1998) and took part in a focus group as a collective. Interview 1 focused on participants' backgrounds and entrée to the classroom, while interview 2 focused on experiences in the field and aspirations for their futures. The focus group was a way to create space for collective meaning-making and, in alignment with narrative inquiry, was driven by the intersectional frame, ultimately helping to achieve what Banks-Wallace (2002) called for: "In particular, the use of data-collection methods grounded in the oral tradition facilitates the bridging of differences and community building among participants and researchers" (p. 424).

FINDINGS

I attempt to equip my students with skills that are unique to their experience and culture but offers them the same opportunity to achieve greatness as students who are not marginalized, we live in a world where minority students and even high performing students of minority races can feel inferior. My goal is to make them very aware of the world that they live in but to believe that greatness is holistically available to everyone even if the odds seem to be stacked against you. —Rashid

This opening quote from research participant Rashid captures the sentiment that ran throughout all interviews and speaks to the strength of an intersectionality-based analytical frame. Participants spoke to all the various identities they assume and that their students and colleagues assumed, and juxtaposed that to what was happening, in real time, in their school buildings, communities, and society as a whole. Through this lens, it was clear that while race and gender played significant roles in their pedagogies, they were also driven by a strong need to effect change in their communities and in their students' lives. Much of this change was centered on helping students see themselves in a light that disrupted the views often held of them—proactively getting students to identify in more self-empowering ways.

Race and gender were also integral in the examples they set for colleagues, as well as in their goals to move the needle on systemic change. That driving force was very clearly rooted in a strong sense of self that resulted from the knowledge they built about their sociocultural and historical legacies. This was a consistent thread that connected all these educators in a very palpable way. Honoring the focus on voice, throughout data analysis,

I leaned on direct quotes from participants to serve as themes that emerged during data analysis and include the following: "What It Looks Like To Be Your Authentic Self," "You Just Wanna Do More Work on the Ground," "Am I an Overseer or Am I a Liberator?," and "I Think That's What This Is About, Leading by Example."

These themes led to the construction of the following theoretical statement: Though Black male special educators sometimes experience their race and gender as the reasons why the full spectrum of their talents and skills are often undervalued, they persevere due to a desire to use education as a platform to challenge the system. Special education as an area of expertise, however, is not as much of a driving force as is remaining rooted in their sociohistorical legacies and a strong sense of self, in order to serve as transformational leaders for students of color.

The analysis and this theoretical statement revealed that for these Black male special educators, a rootedness in their shared sociohistorical identities and legacies, alongside an ever-developing strong sense of self, not only pushed them to enter the field of education, but also motivated them to strive toward becoming transformational leaders in the field. Essentialized experiences as racialized and gendered "others" contributed to their need to actualize their identities in a manner that aligned with how they saw themselves and not how systems defined them.

As such, they consciously shifted away from trying to "prove themselves" as pedagogues and toward a place of owning their self-designed and historically informed truths with pride and dignity. This self-empowerment, as they described it, contributed to their success with their students. To this end, their identities were not just centered on race and gender, but they also connected to the critical consciousness they wanted to elicit in students so they could circumvent the negative ramifications of the many labels society placed on them. As such, a big part of their teacher identity was a sort of activist lens that allowed them to serve as agents of change for the communities they served.

This need to serve students as a form of activism helped them to transmute their disdain for a school system and larger racist society that consistently undermines their efforts into something productive and constructive for themselves and the youth they served. Additionally, experiences with male educators of color, of their past and present, deepened their need to extend their reach, which ultimately translated into them becoming educators and also influenced their view of the changes that are necessary in their work. For example, when it came to preparing teachers for the classroom, Francis asserted, "I think first and foremost, we have to redesign how we're taught to teach. I think even the way we're taught to teach can be very limiting and not really transformational." He also shared the following:

I studied Dr. Lyles because he was a character. He was a father and a teacher at the same time, so he understands that. Hearing his narrative and hearing his story will actually drive me and push me forward—understanding that. We don't have that. There's no Black library of Black male teachers in which you can go back and look at oh, this guy taught in this school. He taught science. We don't see shit like that. There's no coffee book of Black male teachers and pictures of them with a quick page that tells you about them.

Consequently, though their respective goals in the profession were varied, there was great convergence where challenging the status quo was concerned. That is, a consistent critical examination of society and one's place in it was central to their decision to enter the profession and to their pedagogical approaches, as well as to their desire to remain in the profession with a focus on serving as agents of change.

To this end, they perceived a system where the pervasive thought was that instruction should drive culture. That is, by their estimation, the system seemingly operates with the understanding that strong instructional strategy and accountability measures would create a culture of academic achievement. These men, however, sought to turn this notion on its head. They prevailed with the foundation that co-creating a strong culture *with* students would help instruction to come about as an organic, authentic occurrence that naturally produced academic excellence.

Consequently, they balked at what they felt were current expectations of them as male educators of color and led with identity, culture and sociohistorical legacy as a driver for academic and ultimately, community well-being and success. As Kwame stated:

> Culture is part of the learning process. That is why I value it. When you're talking about—there's something specifically about Black and Brown boys and girls. You're talking about a traumatized group, whether we want to acknowledge it or not. The only way that you can really acknowledge trauma is through joy, too, at the same time. I think culture is that joy piece that we need to bring into the classroom.

IMPLICATIONS

Employing an intersectionality-based analysis frame provided space for identity to take center stage in the research, and it also created space for participants to self-identify and self-define along lines of their identity. Just as "In qualitative research, the researcher is seen as the research 'instrument'"

(Harry, 1996, p. 292), a similar thing can be said of teachers—they are the instrument. What this framework helped reveal is a deep need to rest in one's sense of self, that is, one's identity, in order to actualize success in today's teaching context.

This need can be best supported through identity-responsive research and practice (Fenton, 2017). With roots in the feminist epistemologies of intersectionality (Collins, 2015) and an ecological frame (Bronfenbrenner, 1977), this approach acknowledges that as teaching is a socially mediated act (Asante, 1999; Gee, 2000), an individual brings their full self to the work. That is, the person is the instrument for the teaching and learning act, and therefore identity cannot be separated from what happens in classrooms. Accordingly, a level of responsiveness toward this component of the teaching act is necessary for effective policies, and for school and research practices that aim to solve the teacher diversity quandary.

IDENTITY-RESPONSIVE PRACTICES

Just as the field pushes teachers who work with minoritized students to implement culturally responsive and sustaining pedagogies (Gay, 2002; Irvine, 2002; Paris & Alim, 2017), using an identity-responsive approach asks the same of researchers who study minoritized populations. It posits that scholars need to consider not only the identities of the researched, but also researchers' own identities and how they converge with and/or diverge from the identities of others. In the case of research, this helps guard against essentializing marginalized groups (Tefera et al., 2018), as demonstrated in the research study shared herein, and urges the researcher to consider identity construction both from the participant's standpoint (Harding, 2009) and the viewpoint of society, with the aim of examining both the tensions and areas of opportunity that exist at that intersection. This examination then helps ensure that the methodologies, research instruments and questions, and so forth hold space to expose the gaping holes that single (or even double) categories create in analysis (Museus & Griffin, 2011; Tefera et al., 2018).

When it comes to the practice of teacher education, an identity-responsive approach can help provide a space for teachers to probe their identities alongside those who are charged with helping them prepare for the classroom. As hooks (1994) affirmed, "Professors who embrace the challenge of self-actualization will be better able to create pedagogical practices that engage students, providing them with ways of knowing that enhance their capacity to live fully and deeply" (p. 22). Therefore, this approach is fitting not only for minoritized groups, but all groups, since identity is something that is germane to us all in virtually every context of our lives.

Identity-responsive practices also apply to administrators who operate school buildings and have the great responsibility of serving as teacher mentors and instructive leaders of their schools. Principals who utilize identity-responsive frameworks will be pushed to critically examine how their identities intersect with the identities of others (i.e., teachers, students, parents, and community) as well as the systems in which those identities operate. This can help mitigate bias in everything from interpersonal interactions to curricular choices and school culture.

An identity-responsive approach also prioritizes the experiences and voices of those who are most proximate to the issue at hand. In the case of underrepresented populations in the teaching force, this involves engaging minoritized teachers in both the research around this issue and the design of teacher preparation programs. As Francis stated:

> I think the major thing is that we have to redesign. Everyone says universities and teaching colleges need to be redesigned anyway. In regard to being a Black male, you need to be really tailored. Number one, you have to be connected to your past experiences. Number two, not only do you need to understand the content, understand the basics because they are extremely important—I wouldn't take that away. However, I think that looking at the kid holistically and actually studying other Black people—I think one thing—we come from a people that I think thrive off of understanding who has done things before us.

To this end, an identity-responsive approach would call for teacher education programs to engage the literature on Black teachers from education historians (i.e., Siddle Walker, 2001) to understand the best practices that minoritized teachers have found successful with minoritized students over time. For example, the practices of the participants in this study were very well aligned with Siddle Walker's (2001) discussion of the effective practices of Black teachers in the segregated South. This included practices like forming professional coalitions of Black teachers, utilizing deep connections to the communities in which the teachers worked, and linking curriculum with students' real-world needs.

CONCLUSION

Intersectionality as a frame helped give rise to a study that prioritized the voices of the marginalized and allowed room for them to self-identify in ways that demonstrated a need for an identity-responsive approach to solving the teacher diversity issue. This type of approach takes an ecological view of identity and situates it both within the individual, the teaching context, and the society at large. The educators in this study invoked the work of Asante (1999), who stated, "Education is fundamentally a social phenomenon whose ultimate purpose is to socialize the learner; to send a child to school is to prepare that child to become part of a social group" (p. 39). Further, Asante went on to state, "Schools are reflective of the societies that develop them (i.e., a White supremacist-dominated society will develop a White supremacist educational system" (p. 39). It is only with this level of awareness that we can solve issues like teacher diversity from the root cause—racist systems and structures that perpetuate inequities for children of color.

There needs to be increased research that employs critical frameworks like intersectionality to probe the experiences of Black educators in the field, men and women alike. In this manner, the dominant, essentializing narratives around these groups can be disrupted and there can be a more nuanced approach to researching these groups, resulting in a more nuanced view of their experiences and ways of growing as pedagogues. Intersectionality pushes us to value the multiple layers of identities we assume and prioritize the power of hearing from those who not only have extensive professional knowledge, but also hold personal knowledge of what it means to be a marginalized student.

As Vincent, a participant in the study, stated, "They think it's only because you're Black . . ." followed by Francis, who said, ". . . not because you're skilled." With intersectionality at the heart of any research or practice, the entirety of the individuals' identities under examination have no choice but to be raised up as an essential component of the work. Moreover, marginalized groups endure many challenges that are unique to their shared identities; as Brockenbrough (2012) aptly suggested, there are "unique professional and psychosocial challenges that may affect Black men in the profession" (p. 30). Therefore, in addition to attending to a more identity-responsive approach to conducting research, intersectionality should be employed in recommendations like the one from Scott and Rodriguez (2015): "Teacher education programs must be ground zero in modeling critical pedagogy that recognizes the voices of color and the social context of lived experiences to foster and achieve social justice" (p. 712). Not only does this require problematizing the stereotypical beliefs that surround the identities of many who belong to marginalized groups, but it also pushes us to own the fact that we cannot engage in equity work without those who are closest to the equity issue.

We need both critical (Bell, 1995; Freire, 2011; Giroux, 2010) and intersectional (Collins, 1991; Crenshaw, 1991) views to ground us as we combat the issues that inhibit equity in our schools. Absent these, one could argue that structural inequities will persist. As policies fuel the engine on which the educational system runs, those policies need to be informed by research that takes identity into account, not just so that we are clear on who is involved in the problems we aim to solve, but also so we can truly get to the heart of how interlocking identities contend with systems of oppression and how this plays out in classrooms for both teachers and students (Collins, 2015; Freire, 2011). With the type of lens that an intersectionality-based analysis frame provides, we open our eyes, ears and minds to what really matters in our quest for equity: the identities and lived experiences of those our system has failed for far too long.

REFERENCES

Albert Shanker Institute. (2015). *The state of teacher diversity in American education.* http://www.shankerinstitute.org/resource/teacherdiversity

Alkebulan, A. A. (2013). The spiritual and philosophical foundation for African languages. *Journal of Black Studies, 44,* 50–62.

Artiles, A. J. (2013). Untangling the racialization of disabilities: An intersectionality critique across disability models. *DuBois Review, 10*(2), 329–347.

Asante, M. K. (1999). The Afrocentric idea in education. In E. M. Duarte & S. Smith (Eds.), *Foundational perspectives in multicultural education* (pp. 37–49). Longman.

Banerjee, N. (2018). Effects of teacher–student ethnoracial matching and overall teacher diversity in elementary schools on educational outcomes. *Journal of Research in Childhood Education, 32*(1), 94–118.

Banks-Wallace, J. (2002). Talk that talk: Storytelling and analysis rooted in African American oral tradition. *Qualitative Health Research, 12*(3), 410–426.

Bell, D. A. (1995). Who's afraid of critical race theory? *University of Illinois Law Review, 1994*(4), 893–910.

Bristol, T. J., & Martin-Fernandez, J. (2019). *The added value of Latinx and Black teachers for Latinx and Black students: Implications for the reauthorization of the Higher Education Act.* (EdWorkingPaper 19-93). http://www.edworkingpapers.com/ai19-93

Brobbey, G. (2018). Punishing the vulnerable: Exploring suspension rates for students with learning disabilities. *Intervention in School and Clinic, 53*(4), 216–219.

Brockenbrough, E. (2012). Emasculation blues: Black male teachers' perspectives on gender and power in the teaching profession. *Teachers College Record, 114*(5), 1–43.

Brockenbrough, E. (2015). "The discipline stop": Black male teachers and the politics of urban school discipline. *Education and Urban Society, 47*(5), 499–522.

Bronfenbrenner, U. (1977). Toward an experimental ecology of human development. *American Psychologist, 32*(7), 513.

Carbado, D. (2013). Colorblind intersectionality. *Signs, 38*(4), 811–845.

Charmaz, K. (2006). *Constructing grounded theory: A practical guide.* Sage Publications.

Collins, P. H. (1991). *Black feminist thought: Knowledge, consciousness, and the politics of empowerment.* Routledge.

Collins, P. H. (2015). Intersectionality's definitional dilemma. *Annual Review of Sociology, 41,* 1–20.

Collins, P. H., & Bilge, Sirma. (2016). *Intersectionality.* Polity Press.

Crenshaw, K. (1991). Mapping the margins: Intersectionality, identity politics, and violence against women of color. *Stanford Law Review, 43*(6), 1241–1299.

Cresswell, J.W. (1998). *Qualitative inquiry and research design: Choosing among five approaches* (2nd ed.). Sage.

Denzin, N. K., & Lincoln, Y. S. (2005). The discipline and practice of qualitative research. In N. K. Denzin & Y. S. Lincoln (Eds.), *The Sage handbook of qualitative research* (3rd ed., pp. 1–32). Sage.

Engward, H. (2013). Understanding grounded theory. *Nursing Standard, 28*(7), 37–41.

Eubanks, S. C., & Weaver, R. (1999). Excellence through diversity: Connecting the teacher quality and teacher diversity agendas. *Journal of Negro Education, 68*(3), 451–459.

Fenton, P. E. (2017). *Voices at the intersection: Exploring the roles of race and gender in the pedagogies of black male special educators* [Doctoral thesis, University of Miami]. https://eric.ed.gov/?id=ED605354 .

Freire, P. (2011). *Pedagogy of the oppressed* (30th anniversary ed., M. B. Ramos, Trans.). Continuum Publishing Group.

Garcia, S. B., & Ortiz, A. A. (2013). Intersectionality as a framework for transformative research in special education. *Multiple Voices for Ethnically Diverse Exceptional Learners, 13*(2), 32–47.

Gay, G. (2002). Culturally responsive teaching in special education for ethnically diverse students: Setting the stage. *International Journal of Qualitative Studies in Education, 15*(6), 613–629.

Gee, J. P. (2000). Identity as an analytical lens for research in education. *Review of Research in Education, 25*, 99–125.

Gershenson, S., Hart, C. M. D., Lindsay, C. A., & Papageorge, N. W. (2017). The long run effects of same-race teachers (IZA Discussion Paper No. 10630). IZA Institute of Labor Economics. https://www.iza.org/publications/dp/10630

Giroux, H. A. (2010). Rethinking education as the practice of freedom: Paulo Freire and the promise of critical pedagogy. *Policy Futures in Education, 8*(6), 715–721.

Guba, E. G., & Lincoln, Y. S. (2005). Paradigmatic controversies, contradictions, and emerging confluences. In N. K. Denzin & Y. S. Lincoln (Eds.), *The Sage handbook of qualitative research* (3rd ed., pp. 191–215). Sage.

Hamlet, J. D. (2011). Word! The African American oral tradition and its rhetorical impact on American popular culture. *Black History Bulletin, 74*(1), 27–31.

Harding, S. (2009). Standpoint theories: Productively controversial. *Hypatia, 24*(4), 192–200.

Harry, B. (1996). These families, those families: The impact of researcher identities on the research act. *Exceptional Children, 62*(4), 292–301.

hooks, b. (1994). *Teaching to transgress*. New York: Routledge.

Hopson, L., & Lee, E. (2011). Mitigating the effect of family poverty on academic and behavioral outcomes: The role of school climate in middle and high school. *Children and Youth Services Review, 33*(11), 2221–2229.

Irvine, J. J. (2002). *In search of wholeness: African American teachers and their culturally specific classroom practices*. Palgrave.

Kress, J. (2019). *Charting the course to equity: K–12 leaders of color and student success*. California Charter School Association. https://info.ccsa.org/charting-the-course-to-equity

Lewis, C. W., & Toldson, I. (Eds.) (2013). *Black male teachers: Diversifying the United States' teacher workforce* (Advances in Race and Ethnicity in Education, Book 1). Emerald Group.

Lynn, M., & Jennings, M. E. (2009). Power, politics, and critical race pedagogy: A critical race analysis of Black male teachers' pedagogy. *Race Ethnicity and Education, 12*, 173–196.

Merriam, S. B. (2009). *Qualitative research: A guide to design and implementation.* John Wiley & Sons, Inc.

Museus, S., & Griffin, K. (2011). Mapping the margins in higher education: On the promise of intersectionality frameworks in research and discourse. *New Directions for Institutional Research, 2011*(151), 5–13.

Paris, D., & Alim, H. S. (Eds.). (2017). *Culturally sustaining pedagogies: Teaching and learning for justice in a changing world.* Teachers College Press.

Patton, M. Q. (2002). *Qualitative research and evaluation methods* (3rd ed.). Sage.

Rezai-Rashti, G. M., & Martino, W. J. (2010). Black male teachers as role models: Resisting the homogenizing impulse of gender and racial affiliation. *American Educational Research Journal, 47*, 37–64.

Scott, S. V., & Rodriguez, L. F. (2015). "A fly in the ointment": African American male preservice teachers' experiences with stereotype threat in teacher education. *Urban Education, 50*(6), 689–717.

Seidman, I. E. (1998). *Interviewing as qualitative research: A guide for researchers in education and the social sciences* (2nd ed.). Teachers College Press.

Siddle Walker, V. (2000). Valued segregated schools for African American children in the South, 1935-1969: A review of common themes and characteristics. *Review of Educational Research, 70*(3), 253–85.

Sullivan, A., & Bal, A. (2013). Disproportionality in special education: Effects of individual and school variables on disability risk. *Exceptional Children, 79*(4), 475–494.

Sullivan, A., Van Norman, E., & Klingbeil, D. (2014). Exclusionary discipline of students with disabilities: Student and school characteristics predicting suspension. *Remedial and Special Education, 35*(4), 199–210.

Tefera, A., Powers, J., & Fischman, G. (2018). Intersectionality in education: A conceptual aspiration and research imperative. *Review of Research in Education, 42*(1), vii–xvii.

Xu, S., & Connelly, M. (2010). Narrative inquiry for school-based research. *Narrative Inquiry, 20*(2), 349–370.

CHAPTER 8

Translating Research to Local Contexts

Voices of Juvenile Justice-Involved Youth

Wendy Cavendish

The examination of youth perspectives of the juvenile justice system first requires a consideration of the structural framing and political machinations that have influenced the development and evolution of the system itself. This consideration is framed by intersectionality-based analysis (IBA) questions (adapted from Hankivsky et al., 2014, by Samson and Cavendish; see p. 3, Table I.1, this volume) related to how representations of the problem of youth juvenile justice involvement have come about and how the framing of the problem has changed over time and across different spaces. An overview of the historical legal and social reform movements provides the background for discussion of the juvenile justice court and commitment/detention system. The establishment of the United States juvenile court system in 1899 was informed by public opinion and a resultant policy shift that was youth-centered. This shift resulted in an approach whereby court case dispositions were rendered based on the needs of youth, in contrast with sentencing based on "seriousness of offense" as occurred in adult court (Hinton et al., 2007). Thus, the juvenile justice system was founded on a perspective that some youth (generally White, middle-class youth) who violated some aspect of the law can be supported or rehabilitated (Garascia, 2005). This focus continued for decades and was reinforced by social reform movements in the 1920s and 1930s that recognized the developmental difference of childhood from adulthood. However, researchers have noted that the developmental distinction of childhood was not (and has not been) extended to immigrant or Black youth in the juvenile justice courts and systems (Pickett & Chiricos, 2012).

An evolution of the criminal justice system took place when adult and youth crime rates rose substantially in the 1980s and 1990s (Snyder, 2011), spurring tough-on-crime policies throughout the country (Garascia, 2005). These legislative changes occurred in most states and included a shift to more punitive sanctions and harsher sentencing for youth offenders, including the substantial increase in the transfer of youth to the adult criminal justice system during this time (Hinton et al., 2007). A central assumption in the field is that the politicization of crime led to criminalizing the juvenile justice system in spite of research that demonstrates the harm this does to youth (e.g., Mears et al., 2007).

JUVENILE JUSTICE FOR WHOM?

In considering the representations of the juvenile justice system response to youth crime and its effectiveness in reducing reoffending by juveniles, it is critical to consider the framing of the problem and the resultant policies and practices used to address it. It has been argued that even at its inception, the juvenile justice system was used in efforts to subordinate low-income, immigrant, and Black youth (Mears et al., 2007; Pickett & Chiricos, 2012). The adultification of Black and Brown youth in courts and the criminal justice system (Pickett & Chiricos, 2012) is aligned with the more punitive focus and criminalization of the juvenile system since the 1980's. This process of adultification has been maintained as documented in the literature on "symbolic threat" whereby crime is equated with race (Hogan et al., 2005). This research posits that Black males remain a "particular target for punitive sanctions" because they are perceived to "be a potent threat to social order" by the White middle and upper classes (Mears et al., 2007, p. 233).

A consideration of the impact of the punitive legislative shift provides an opportunity to address the IBA question related to how existing policies address, maintain, or create inequities between different groups and answers how groups are differentially affected by the representation of the "problem" of juvenile crime. Disparate contact and treatment based on race and ethnicity have been consistently recorded at all levels of the criminal justice system, from disproportionate arrest rates to differentially harsh sentencing (Harrell & Davis, 2020; Ward, 2015). Currently, Black youth are more than three times as likely as White youth to be referred to criminal court (Puzzanchera & Hockenberry, 2018). The adultification of youth also extends beyond just race to gendered differential contact with the criminal justice system, particularly for Black girls impacted by intersectional systems of oppression in schools, communities, and the criminal justice system (Epstein, Blake, & Gonzalez, 2017). For example, Black girls are 15% of the school-age population but represent 37% of the arrests made in schools in 2014 (Epstein et al., 2017).

The transition of youth from juvenile justice and correctional settings back into schools, families, and communities, a process alternately termed youth reentry or community reintegration, has received limited empirical research attention. However, the criminalization of Black and Brown youth is often exacerbated by the deficit framing (criminogenic risk) used in the limited research on juvenile reentry from facilities into schools, families, and communities. Most of the research has been focused on factors impacting recidivism (rearrest rates) that include notions of criminogenic propensity. This emphasis is evidenced in the use of "risk" or "criminogenic" assessments widely administered during juvenile commitment and prior to release and community reentry. For example, in Florida, the site of the study shared in this chapter, the Florida Department of Juvenile Justice identifies the Prevention Assessment Tool and the Community Assessment Tool as a "cornerstone" of reentry efforts used to "assist Juvenile Probation Officers . . . in determining a youth's level of risk to re-offend" and identify "areas of highest criminogenic need" (Florida Department of Juvenile Justice, 2019).

Juvenile recidivism rates are not calculated nationally, but most reports suggest a rate of 55–60% (FDJJ, 2019), and there is limited empirical research that conclusively identifies factors related to successful juvenile reentry. The difficulty in obtaining accurate descriptive information on youth program performance during and after commitment to residential juvenile justice facilities is also related to disparities in states' departments of education and departments of juvenile justice collection and reporting of data (Livsey, Sickmund, & Sladky, 2009). The fact that child welfare, education, employment data,, and juvenile justice information systems are rarely integrated (e.g., Herz et al., 2010) has made it difficult to accurately track outcomes for juvenile justice-involved students. What we do know, based on rearrest rates, is that the targeting of "criminogenic risk" that reflects a deficit-based, punitive versus rehabilitative stance is not effective.

RESEARCH ON JUVENILE REENTRY

Bouffard and Bergseth (2008) reported that there is a lack of empirical support for commonly applied "community restraint" models of juvenile reentry that include surveillance through probation contact and monitoring. They suggest that "intervention" models of juvenile reentry that provide employment, academic, and therapeutic supports are potentially more impactful than community restraint. However, they note that most intervention or program models examined in the research are "plagued by a predominance of null effect" primarily related to "shortcomings in the implementation of treatment/service aspects of the program" (p. 297). Early evaluations of community reentry programs have been criticized for narrowly focusing on criminogenic risk as related to recidivism and for not focusing on treatment programming to isolate individual components that may be effective. More recently, the Office of Juvenile Justice and Delinquency Prevention (OJJDP), an agency of the U.S. Department of Justice, also reported that the research on the effectiveness of juvenile reentry programs has produced meager and conflicting results (OJJDP, 2017). However, the OJJDP, while readily noting the mental health, education, employment, and family socioeconomic needs of juvenile justice-involved youth, continues to support a comprehensive reentry model that integrates intervention strategies but also community restraint including intensive supervision, electronic monitoring, house arrest, and regular drug testing.

Although the limited research on juvenile reentry points to a need for wraparound community, education, and therapeutic support (e.g., Bouffard & Bergseth, 2008), the criminal and juvenile justice systems do not generally fund these community resources. However, most states require a community restraint model of supervision via probation post-release for almost all juvenile justice-involved youth, and state and county juvenile justice systems fund the salaries of Juvenile Probation Officers (JPOs). The system emphasis on community restraint has not reduced youth recidivism using this model (OJJDP, 2017). Thus, it is critical to engage the perspectives and voices of youth who have experienced this system approach to inform recommendations for changes in policy and practice.

In order to focus on a social justice approach to juvenile justice research, I applied the IBA frame to my own research in reflecting on the questions, "What knowledge, values, and experiences do you bring to this area? What social determinants affect your perspective?" I consider my own positionality related to juvenile justice policy and research. I am motivated to work and research in this field because I experienced the system from the inside, having spent 14 months in a juvenile residential facility as a teenager. I acknowledge that I entered this field as a researcher biased in my perspective that the juvenile justice system is most often dysfunctional and harmful to youth. My 13 years of experience as a research partner with criminal justice-focused governmental and community agencies have also influenced my views of the potential of multiagency and cross-program collaboration based on witnessing the committed, caring, and authentic work on behalf of the youth by some community partners and stakeholders. Also, as a White female faculty member, I am cognizant of how much power and privilege I now bring to all of my interactions with those within the system, and although I maintain a more balanced perspective, I remain deeply suspicious in my interactions with criminal justice agents. I acknowledge that I am impacted by the powerlessness of my previous experience and the abuses of power by those within the system who often exploited my age and gender in their enactment of their power.

The purpose of the research reported in this chapter is to highlight the voices of youth themselves related to what policies or practices implemented by the juvenile justice system support or hinder their progress toward successful community reintegration.

METHOD

The 19 participants were drawn from a group of youth who were involved in a county reentry program immediately following release from residential juvenile commitment centers. The program's broad goal was to provide case management supports across systems for education, employment, counseling, independent living, and restitution (conditions of probation) in order to decrease recidivism of youth in the first year post-release. The demographics of the 19 youth were consistent with the disproportionate representation of Black youth in the criminal justice system. The youth were 74% male and 26% female; 76% Black, 15% White, and 9% Latinx; and the youth ranged in age from 13 to 19 years old (mean age was 17 years, 1 month). In addition, 35% of the youth were also served in special education.

Semi-structured interviews to probe youth perceptions of practices that were contributing to or hindering their progress toward community reintegration (defined by the juvenile justice system as meeting all requirements of post-release probation) were conducted in three focus groups. Interview questions included items such as, "How has your past involvement with the juvenile justice system affected you? Impacted your goals? Hurt you? Helped you?" and "What activities or experiences do you think are helping you most toward your goals?"

Each focus group lasted approximately one hour. Audio recordings of the focus groups were transcribed verbatim. The qualitative analysis consisted of a 3-step constant comparative coding process (Charmaz, 2006) that included an initial process using an inductive coding approach that resulted in the identification of 247 open codes. In the second step, the codes were analyzed deductively and sorted into categories of support or hindrance. The codes were then sorted into 10 "families" of grouped codes. Finally, the last coding step resulted in the emergence of three thematic categories. A truncated version of the findings is presented below.

FINDINGS

The three thematic categories that emerged are: Opportunities and effective supports; social–emotional challenges to reentry; and procedural challenges to reentry. Youth discussed their experiences during commitment and the relationship of these experiences to successes and effective supports upon returning to home and school environments as well as challenges in meeting community reentry requirements set by the juvenile court.

Theme 1: Opportunities and Supports

The youth identified supports that were provided by the reentry program as including help obtaining identification and Social Security cards, rides to school, and job assistance. Most youth noted that the case managers in the program were committed and didn't give up on them even when they "ignored texts" or "didn't show" for meetings with the program staff. One of the youth stated of the program staff, "To be real with you, people here—like I tell them all the time, they like my second mom." Other youth noted that they primarily sought support from family, including mothers, older siblings, and older cousins. Regarding social networks, most of the youth discussed the need to "cut off" old friends (from prior to juvenile commitment) for reasons such as, "They're not my real friends" and "They just trying to drag me down." One youth stated, "The best thing I could do is just focus on myself."

Most of the youth noted that they were motivated to not return to juvenile commitment and that staying home, keeping to themselves, and going to school kept them out of trouble and helped them reach their goals. All of the youth articulated specific goals related to education and employment, including the desire to obtain a diploma and have careers such as electrician, business owner, mechanic, and lawyer. However, they also generally expressed that meeting immediate goals such as obtaining employment and working toward a high school diploma or GED was challenging given other court obligations such as community service hours, restitution requirements, and curfew.

Theme 2: Social–Emotional Challenges to Successful Reentry

Several youth shared negative experiences during commitment that they were still grappling with upon return to their home community. Most youth talked about the stress of managing emotions during commitment such as managing anger when items were stolen and handling perceived disrespect during commitment. They noted that their responses to this often resulted in fights that extended their time in commitment. Two youth discussed the stress of being in adult jail in a different county, with one female stating, "[The facility] was known as a racist jail" and that other inmates "knew I wasn't from that county . . . so would mess with me." This resulted in her being put on lockdown for 23 hours a day. Other stressors noted included family loss during commitment. Two of the 19 youth lost their grandmothers while they were committed. This had both immediate and lasting emotional impact; as one female noted, "My grandmother was like my mother," and that she expected when she "got out" that she would be with her grandmother. She noted, "I didn't know how sick she was . . . . When staff told [me] about her death, they had to hold me down." The male youth stated that "thinking about how [my grandmother] died would probably land me back in jail" and that "dealing with the stress of her death was confusing." Several youth stated that the program was trying to arrange for therapy for them, but it was difficult with scheduling and cost as it wasn't required as part of conditions of probation.

Many of the youth also identified current personal and family challenges that impacted their ability to complete court-required conditions of their community reentry probation. The ongoing stress of family loss and conflict was consistently noted. Many youth discussed the need to provide support for their families as motivation to stay out of jail. One youth talked about his sister's recent arrest and that he needed to stay out because "I'm the youngest and the only boy. So I felt like when I'm gone, my mom gone. It's automatic." Another mentioned that he had to "be strong" for his mom, as his brothers were arrested shortly before he himself was released. He noted that he "doesn't want my mom to have to work forever" and that he had "to be strong in mind to tighten up and not follow in [his] brother's footsteps." He noted, "It was easy money [for his brothers], but not good money. I got to go the long way."

Theme 3: Procedural Challenges to Reentry

All youth noted procedural challenges in meeting all the requirements of the conditions of their probation post-release, even with program support. This was mainly due to challenges in school enrollment; balancing limited employment earnings, independent living costs, and restitution; and managing family and probation commitments with curfew requirements. Some students had been successfully reenrolled in their home schools upon return to the community. However, other students noted challenges with enrollment related to having so few credits and thus being considerably overage for their grade. Some youth were taking GED classes as a result, and most noted feeling as though this option was a good fit for their needs. A few youth noted resistance from their home schools for enrollment; as one student stated, "It's hard when you already got a reputation." Regardless of type of school program enrolled in (general education or special education), many youth noted the need for a tutor for academic support, but not having transportation if they stayed after school for support was an obstacle. School attendance challenges included family obligations such as missing school due to mother's hospitalization, or the illness of a youth's 10-month-old son. This youth noted being re-arrested for a probation violation for not attending school during his son's illness.

The myriad probation requirements youth were expected to simultaneously meet as conditions of their probation included school attendance, employment, restitution, community service hours, and curfews. Youth also noted transportation as a challenge, as they were mainly dependent on public transportation (in a very large county with mainly public busses as transportation options) or catching rides from friends, family, or program staff. One youth noted that he was fired from his job for inconsistent arrival times, being late or clocking in early.

As several youth were living independently (or in temporary housing provided by the program), employment and earning money were key concerns. However, many youth were limited in employment options when also required to attend full-time school or due to curfew requirements. For example, one youth had both a high school attendance requirement and a 7:00 P.M. curfew, making his employment options limited to weekends only. This in turn placed him behind in restitution payments required by probation. Most of the youth expressed that the competing requirements of probation were a "setup." One youth stated, "We are like animals on a leash." There were varying experiences with the level of adherence required by probation officers, with some youth expressing, "It's not right, they'll violate you out of pettiness," and another stating, "Some things with probation are legitimate, others are ridiculous."

IMPLICATIONS

The findings presented represent the voices of juvenile justice-involved youth and as such, address the IBA consideration related to research as reflective of the perspectives and self-identified needs of affected groups. In this study, youth identified opportunities and challenges in successfully meeting requirements for community reentry. Their own words highlight the need for provision of intervention supports in education, employment, and mental health within the community restraint model they were experiencing. Although all youth were participating in a juvenile reentry program, resources were fully provided only for probation monitoring, not for support services. For example, youth with intensive mental health needs were not provided access to a therapist under court or reentry program funding. While the youth expressed appreciation for program case manager support in helping them navigate the school and employment probation requirements, they were still grappling with stress and grief experienced during and after commitment.

The criminogenic risk focus of the juvenile reentry system does not consider the ways in which youth and families may be impacted by structural inequities such as limited opportunity due to race and low-income status as well as racially biased policing and criminal justice processing at every stage.

The youth who shared their perspectives were primarily Black youth from low-income communities who are now also saddled with the label of "juvenile offender" by all the systems they are required to interact with (school system, employers, probation officers). So in applying the IBA framing question of "How are interactions at individual levels of experience linked to social institutions and processes of power?," one must return to the youths' expressed perceptions that "probation is a setup." Of note, among youth who are rearrested for technical violations of probations (not a new offense but violation of technical probation requirements such as skipping school, missing a JPO appointment, or having a dirty drug test), more than 66% are Black or Brown youth (Coalition for Juvenile Justice, 2014).

These youth are impacted by systems that are additionally not welcoming because of the youth's "offender" label (beyond race and income status), and thus they experience obstacles at the complex intersection of multiple labels/identities affected by more than one systemic challenge (Wallace, 2012). The school system is not welcoming to them ("It's hard when you got a reputation"), and they have academic support needs not supported by system resources (special education, credit recovery, and tutoring needs), but the juvenile justice system mandates that they must reenroll in school and regularly attend or they are subject to rearrest for violation of probation.

Many of the youth expressed mental health needs related to significant trauma and loss (as well as dehumanizing harm during commitment such as the 23-hour lockdown for 30 days experienced by one youth), but the juvenile justice system does not systematically provide resources for these supports. The youth are also subject to contradictory requirements within the system itself via restitution and employment requirements as conditions of probation that also requires full-time school enrollment and a curfew. The punitive community restraint model of juvenile reentry does seem to be, in fact, a "setup" to keep low-income Black youth subordinated via commitment/incarceration.

It is important to acknowledge that this research is not a phenomenological inquiry or auto-ethnography, so I am providing only my interpretation of the youths' perspectives. However, the explicit consideration of the IBA framing questions at all stages of the research allows for expanded consideration of the "problem" addressed by the research. This research provides youth perspectives that reveal inequities and intersecting systems of oppression (juvenile justice, criminal justice, and education systems) experienced based on race, class, and gender. The youths' voices support a critical need to move from community restraint approaches (reducing recidivism) to a consideration of how to best support youth and families with wraparound needs living in dysfunctional systems that differentially impact Black, Brown, poor, and labeled (delinquent/offender) youth (e.g., Cole & Cohen, 2013). The youth in juvenile commitment centers and adult jails who are returning to our schools and communities are children and adolescents in need of supports, not "offenders" requiring punitive community restraint.

REFERENCES

Bouffard, J., & Bergseth, K. (2008). The impact of reentry services on juvenile offenders' recidivism. *Youth Violence and Juvenile Justice, 6*(3), 295–318.

Charmaz, K. (2006). *Constructing grounded theory.* Sage.

Coalition for Juvenile Justice. (2014). *Disproportionate minority contact and status offenses.* Emerging Issues Policy Series, 2. https://www.juvjustice.org/sites/default/files/resource-files/DMC%20Emerging%20Issues%20Policy%20Brief%20Final_0.pdf

Cole, H., & Cohen, R. (2013). Breaking down barriers: A case study of juvenile justice personnel perspectives on school reentry. *The Journal of Correctional Education, 64*(1), 13–35.

Epstein, R., Blake, J., & Gonzalez, T. (2017). *Girlhoods interrupted: The erasure of Black girls' childhood.* Georgetown Law Center on Poverty and Inequality. https://www.law.georgetown.edu/poverty-inequality-center/wp-content/uploads/sites/14/2017/08/girlhood-interrupted.pdf

Florida Department of Juvenile Justice. (2019). *Risk assessment tools.* http://www.djj.state.fl.us/partners/our-approach/RA

Garascia, J. (2005). The price we are willing to pay for punitive justice in the juvenile detention system: Mentally ill delinquents and their disproportionate share of the burden. *Indiana Law Journal, 80*(2), 489–503.

Harrell, E., & Davis, E. (2020). *Contacts between police and the public, 2018 – Statistical tables.* Bureau of Justice Statistics, U.S. Department of Justice. https://www.bjs.gov/content/pub/pdf/cbpp18st.pdf

Herz, D. C., Ryan, J. P., & Bilchik, S. (2010). Challenges facing crossover youth: An examination of juvenile-justice decision making and recidivism. *Family Court Review, 48*(2), 305–321.

Hinton, W., Sims, P., Adams, A., & West, C. (2007). Juvenile justice: A system divided. *Criminal Justice Policy Review, 18*(4), 466–483.

Hogan, M., Armstrong, G., & Rodriguez, N. (2005). Effects of individual and contextual characteristics on preadjudication detention of juvenile delinquents. *Justice Quarterly, 22*, 521–539.

Livsey, S., Sickmund, M., & Sladky, A. (2009). *Juvenile residential facility census, 2004: Selected findings.* Juvenile Offenders and Victims: National Report Series. Department of Justice, Office of Juvenile Justice & Delinquency Prevention. https://www.ncjrs.gov/pdffiles1/ojjdp/222721.pdf

Mears, D., Hay, C., Gertz, M., & Mancini, C. (2007). Public opinion and the foundation of the juvenile court. *Criminology, 45*(1), 223–251.

Office of Juvenile Justice and Delinquency Prevention. (2017). *Literature review: Model programs guide on juvenile reentry.* Author.

Pickett, J., & Chiricos, T. (2012). Controlling other people's children: Racialized views of delinquency and Whites' punitive attitudes toward juvenile offenders. *Criminology, 50*(3), 673–696.

Puzzanchera, C., & Hockenberry, S. (2018). *National disproportionate minority contact databook*. National Center for Juvenile Justice for the Office of Juvenile Justice and Delinquency Prevention.

Snyder, H. (2011). *Arrests in the United States, 1980–2009*. Bureau of Justice Statistics, U.S. Department of Justice. https://www.bjs.gov/content/pub/pdf/aus8009.pdf

Wallace, P. (2012). Juvenile justice and education: Identifying leverage points and recommendations for reform for reentry in Washington, DC. *Georgetown Journal on Poverty Law and Policy, XIX*(1), 159–172.

Ward, G. (2015). The slow violence of state organized race crime. *Theoretical Criminology, 19*(3), 299–314. doi.org/10.1177/1362480614550119

CHAPTER 9

Indigenous Learning Lab

Inclusive Knowledge Production and Systemic
Design Toward Indigenous Prolepsis

Aydin Bal, Aaron Bird Bear, Dosun Ko, and Linda Orie

> In my judgment, the time has arrived when we should definitely make up
> our minds to recognize the Indian as an individual and not as a member of
> a tribe. The General Allotment Act is a mighty pulverizing engine to break
> up the tribal mass. It acts directly upon the family and the individual. . . . In
> the schools the education should be elementary and largely industrial. The
> need of higher education among the Indians is very, very limited. . . . During
> the change of treatment inevitable hardships will occur; every effort should
> be made to minimize these hardships; but we should not because of them
> hesitate to make the change.
>
> —Theodore Roosevelt (1901)

For at least 13,500 years, humans, and the Indigenous nations, languages,
and cultures they created over thousands of years, have existed in what is
now known as the United States of America. The opening quote from a
1901 speech by then-President Theodore Roosevelt highlights the United
States's policies of assimilation and termination that were created to eradicate Native American family and tribal ties, languages, and cultures and that
were enacted in a framework of settler colonialism. Scholars of settler colonialism say that settler colonialism strives for the dissolution of Indigenous
societies by establishing a new colonial society on seized land with the elimination of Indigenous societies as an organizing principle (Wolfe, 2006). In
what would become the United States of America, approximately 90–95%
of the Indigenous population perished from disease, warfare, forced internment, and youth incarceration in boarding schools. At the time of President
Roosevelt's speech in 1901, only 237,000 Native Americans remained alive
in the United States (Smith, 2017). The 2.9 million tribal citizens alive in
the U.S. today, who comprise 573 Indigenous nations with 169 different

languages, are direct descendants of the 237,000 Native Americans who survived into the 20th century. Native Americans make up less than 1% of the U.S. population in the 21st century. As for how American Indian and Alaska Native youth continue to make meaning of settler colonialism and its outcomes, the rate of suicide of Native American youth is 2.5 times higher than their peers'—the highest youth suicide rate among all races/ethnicities in the country (National Congress of American Indians, 2020). Through the education system, Native Americans experienced downward assimilation and cultural genocide (Wolfe, 2006). Native Americans are in fact not racial minorities, but rather are tribal citizens meeting constitutional criteria for citizenship in sovereign Indigenous nations with treaty-based relationships with the U.S. federal government, and as such, Native Americans are political minorities as determined by U.S. Supreme Court decisions and various state supreme court decisions such as *United States v. Antelope*, 430 U.S. 641 (1977); *Morton v. Mancari*, 417 U.S. 535 (1974); *Regents of the University of California v. Bakke*, 438 U.S. 265 (1978); and *Dairyland Greyhound Park v. Doyle*, 295 Wis.2d 1 (2006). However, in and through formal schooling, Native Americans have become racialized in U.S. society.

In the U.S. schools, Native American youth experience exclusionary disciplinary actions more frequently and severely along with youth from other racially minoritized communities, namely African American and Latinx students (Bal, Betters-Bubon, & Fish, 2019; Orfield et al., 2014; Skiba et al., 2002). Disproportionality in school discipline is a result of historically accumulated contradictions arising from racist settler colonial society, such as deep and widening disparities in health, justice, housing, and wealth. Disproportionality as a systemic crisis impacts the lives of youth, families, educators, and society as a whole (Gregory et al., 2010). Disciplinary exclusion brings about long-term detrimental academic, behavioral, and life outcomes. Exclusionary discipline may yield loss of instructional time, academic disengagement, and low achievement (Gregory et al., 2010; Skiba et al., 2014). It is also correlated with recurring behavioral problems and drop-out, and acts as a doorway to the "school-to-prison pipeline" mediated by minoritized youth's increased likelihood of involvement in the juvenile justice system (Kim et al., 2010; Morris, 2016).

Racial disproportionality in school discipline is a contextually situated problem whose patterns and predictors change from one social, historical, and spatial context to another (Bal, 2017). As a persistent inequity issue, disproportionality requires intersectionality-based analysis of how the intersectional matrix of different social markers (re)produces privilege and marginalization in sociohistorically produced spaces (Artiles, 2019; Bal, 2017). The intersections of multiple student-, teacher-, school-, and neighborhood-level factors generate complex landscapes of racial disproportionality. Students' race, gender, academic achievement, or family income; classroom management practices; administrators' disciplinary philosophy; schools' demographic composition; and geographic locations (e.g., urban, suburban, or urbanizing) constitute kaleidoscopic landscapes of disproportionality (Welsh & Little, 2018). As a systemic contradiction, addressing disproportionality demands joint, collaborative efforts beyond disjointed initiatives and fragmented division of labor in education systems. Addressing this enduring inequity requires a situated, intersectional understanding of multiple interacting factors and activity systems to help develop localized solutions in response to school communities' diverse experiences, needs, and goals.

In schools, disproportionality generates a double bind for education leaders, teachers, and families that is "a societally essential dilemma which cannot be resolved through separate individual actions alone—but in which joint, co-operative actions can push a historically new form of activity into emergence" (Engeström, 1987, p. 165). However, a majority of disproportionality studies rely on descriptive analyses focused on problem identification (Artiles, 2011; Cavendish et al., 2014). Despite a conceptual emphasis on expanded family/community engagement, critical dialogue on how intersections of race, class, and ability inform disciplinary practices and educational opportunities is needed to address racial disproportionality (Carter et al., 2016).

Intersectionality can be instrumental for developing ecologically valid, community-led, inclusive, and sustainable systemic transformation efforts to eradicate racial disproportionality. Intersectionality should not be solely used as a conceptual tool for making visible the complexities of identities of individuals from nondominant communities for patronizing goals of so-called "critical" academicians or critical critics (Marx & Engels, 2017) such as "giving voices to voiceless" or "representing the non-dominant communities' interests." If we stay in that idealistic, individualist, and cognitivist realm, intersectionality can turn into yet another trending concept of the day. As a result, this approach generates abstraction on abstraction without concrete, strategic, coordinated, and field-tested actions. It will serve only to benefit academicians (e.g., publications and promotions) without any concrete changes in the lives of nondominant communities. It is vital to remember that Crenshaw (1991) developed her work to make actual changes in a specific activity system where race, gender, and class domination converge (law) for a specific group (Black women) within a specific sociospatial context (the United States of America) to achieve concrete goals (addressing violence and discrimination that Black women face in social and institutional spheres). Using intersectionality in education demands then that education researchers should engage in knowledge production side by side with (not for) historically marginalized communities for the purpose of transforming unjust systems that reproduce disparities in educational opportunities (Bal, 2017). In education sciences and social sciences in general, the question of how to stimulate and maintain situated, intersectional problem identification and collaborative problem-solving processes with local stake-holders for systemic transformation has lingered.

In this chapter we will address this gap and present *how* we have ad-dressed this critical gap in the literature. Since 2011, our research team has conducted a multisite formative intervention, *Learning Lab*, in public schools (urban, urbanizing, and rural) in the United States to address racial disproportionality with local stakeholders (families, students, educators, policymakers, and community members), especially those from historical-ly marginalized groups, contributing to knowledge production and prob-lem-solving activities in education practice and research (Bal, 2011). We will present a new model of Learning Lab, *Indigenous Learning Lab*, as a case in point. In partnership with an Anishinaabe tribal nation, tribal people, and White school staff, our research team is working at a rural public high school to facilitate local stakeholders' situated, intersectional understanding of how race, critical historicity of White settler colonialism, and cultural genocide (re)produce and perpetuate racialized outcome dis-parities, which is vital to the design and implementation of a culturally re-sponsive, schoolwide behavioral support system. More specifically, in this chapter we will address the following questions: (1) how to facilitate an inclusive problem-solving and systemic design activity of local stakehold-ers for systemic transformation in schools; (2) how to unite and sustain inclusive problem-solving teams of people with diverse and often opposing histories, practices, and goals for systemic transformation.

LEARNING LAB: AN INCLUSIVE FUTURE-MAKING PROCESS TOWARD PARTICIPATORY JUSTICE

From a dialectical perspective, disproportionality is a cyclical systemic crisis that offers an important opportunity to critically examine existing prac-tices and transform schools that generate and perpetuate racial dispari-ties (Bal, 2017). The Learning Lab methodology provides a collaborative problem-solving and design focus in which local stakeholders engage in "a process-oriented examination of marginalization and domination pro-cesses in order to disrupt those unjust processes, and, in turn, outcomes in local contexts" (Bal, 2017, p. 7). Learning Lab taps into intersectional funds of knowledge, epistemologies, distributed expertise, and agency of local stakeholders, notably those historically excluded from the school's de-cisionmaking process (e.g., parents of color, immigrant families, students, paraprofessionals, community representatives) for attaining what Bal (2012) called *participatory social justice*. Participatory social justice manifests when historically marginalized communities continue to access knowledge production and decisionmaking in civic activities (e.g., education, urban planning, and health care) and academia (Bal, 2012). Learning Lab employs historical epistemology to reveal often-invisible contradictions in a school system that is constantly evolving. Anishinaabe participants are encouraged to bring collective experiences of struggles, frustrations, and resistance in the past to inform present innovations in design as they endeavor to author the future of their school together with the school staff.

Learning Lab members follow a cycle of expansive learning actions consisting of forming the group, questioning, analyzing (empirical and historical) and modeling, testing, and stabilizing new solutions to resolve the systemwide problems of practice (Bal et al., 2018; Engeström, 2016; Engeström & Sannino, 2010, see Figure 9.1). Expansive learning actions aim to make often-invisible systemic injustice visible and generate qualitative transformation in the school system through exercising the school community's collective, transformative agency. Members meet for 8–10 consecutive sessions with unique agendas aligned with a cycle of expansive learning action. Two or three members are selected as school or community liaisons. Before each meeting, the research team meets with liaisons to discuss the previous meeting and the agenda of the upcoming meeting. The process seeks to facilitate and sustain a systemic transformation led and owned by stakeholders.

Figure 9.1. The Cycle of Systemic Change (Adapted from Engeström & Sannino, 2010)

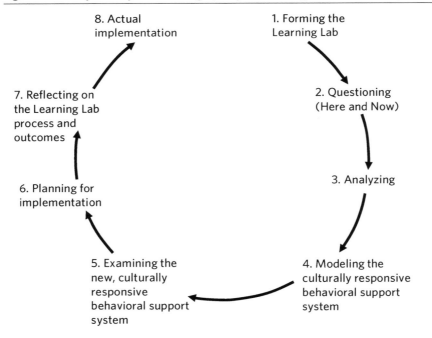

Learning Lab is a formative intervention methodology (Sannino et al., 2016). Formative interventions aim to facilitate the remediation of dysfunctional systems with local practitioners through collaborative epistemic inquiry into systemic contradictions generating paralyzing disturbances in organizations and social movements (Engeström & Sannino, 2010). The collaborative examination of inner systemic contradictions (e.g., racial disparities in discipline or teaching during the COVID-19 pandemic) and the creation of new instrumentality aims to resolve daily disturbances and conflicts resulting from the inner contradictions. Learning Lab facilitates the transformation and expansion of the school discipline system's object (e.g., transforming the punishment and exclusion of students with challenging behaviors into prevention and inclusive, positive support for *all* students and adults in a school community).

The expansive cycle toward systemic transformation starts with the formation of an inclusive problem-solving team of 10–15 members of the school community as a task force (Bal, 2018). The team represents the multiple experiences, needs, and goals within the school community. During the initial meetings, members question the existing school outcomes and practices as well as analyze root causes that generate and perpetuate racialized outcome disparities. Members are encouraged to record discipline-related incidents that they experience or witness. They then examine the school's behavioral outcome data (e.g., ODRs, suspensions, expulsions), disaggregated by race, gender, family income, or disability status to unveil previously invisible disparities in aggregated data with an intersectional lens. Also, members interrogate seemingly "race-neutral" institutional policies (e.g., codes of conduct) and schoolwide behavioral expectations and disciplinary action logistics such as Infinite Campus (school data management software). These artifacts function as a mirror to the data, stimulating problem identification as participants question the existing system.

Once members develop a situated understating of racialized behavioral outcomes in their school, they move to engage in a root cause analysis. Facilitators introduce mapping out the existing school discipline system (e.g., a flow chart showing how a behavioral disturbance in the class is handled and who is responsible for what) as an analytic tool. This map of the school's existing discipline system functions as a secondary stimulus that helps members to move from problem identification to problem solving. This movement is important because a majority of disproportionality research and education research in general exclusively focus on problem identification (Cavendish et al., 2014). Through empirical and historical analyses, members move across multiple time scales (among the past, the present, and the future), within multiple geographical contexts (from neighborhood to city to state to nation), to analyze the school's discipline system from diverse perspectives.

Once daily disturbances, breakdowns, conflicts, and dilemmas that students, educators, and families experience related to the inner systemic contradiction in the school are analyzed and visually represented through mapping out the school's existing discipline system, Learning Lab facilitators form small groups with three or four members and ask each small group to design their ideal system. The facilitators ask each group to discuss the purpose of the existing system that was just mapped out, identify problems, and brainstorm possible improvements. The next step is to merge the existing system with the ideal system, including newly emerged solutions. This new system is designated as a *culturally responsive* behavioral support system. The new system is rigorously examined to identify its utility, dynamics, and limitations. Finally, members work on an implementation plan for the next school year and reflect on the whole Learning Lab process.

So far Learning Lab has been implemented at six public schools in the United States. Five Learning Lab schools were able to design a new culturally responsive system based on their communities' unique and diverse needs, resources, and goals. Each implementation has expanded and refined the Learning Lab design. Currently, Learning Lab is being implemented in multiple schools and school districts internationally. Our research team is currently working with six schools in two school districts in the states of Florida and Wisconsin. In the current Learning Labs, we will be working with schools for 3 years for system design (Year 1), implementation (Year 2), and sustainability (Year 3 and more).

In what follows, we present a detailed description of a new Learning Lab, *Indigenous Learning Lab*, formed at a rural high school, Northwoods High. The school is located in a rural border town in Northern Wisconsin, within a Midwest geopolitical area referred to as the "Deep North" by some American Indians. The school serves multiple counties, including an American Indian reservation inhabited by a tribal nation of Anishinaabe people. Today the Anishinaabe of Wisconsin comprise six distinct tribal nations from the Great Lakes Band of Lake Superior Ojibwe: The Bad River Band of Lake Superior Chippewa, the Lac Courte Oreilles Band of Lake Superior Chippewa, the Red Cliff Band of Lake Superior Chippewa, the St. Croix Chippewa, the Sokaogon (Mole Lake) Chippewa, and the Lac du Flambeau Band of Lake Superior Chippewa.

Indigenous Learning Lab addresses the longstanding disproportionality in school discipline that the Anishinaabe community as a racialized, political minority group continually experiences at Northwoods High. The ultimate goal of Indigenous Learning Lab is systemic transformation for collectively creating positive, inclusive, and supportive behavioral systems for all students and adults. Indigenous Learning Lab utilizes histories, practices, goals, and agencies of American Indian students, families, and community members. Moreover, Indigenous Learning Lab incorporates Indigenous epistemologies into the collective problem-solving and design processes. Indigenous Learning Lab follows three indigenous epistemological principles: *respect, revitalization,* and *reconciliation* (McInnes, 2019). Below, we socially and spatially contextualize the project.

DESIGNING THE FUTURE: INDIGENOUS LEARNING LAB

Settler Colonial Landscape in Wisconsin

Figure 9.2 includes the natural boundary between Minnesota and Wisconsin, the Mississippi River, a defining boundary of U.S. Indian Removal policy, which held that all Indigenous people east of the Mississippi must be forcibly relocated to west of the Mississippi. As of March 2020, the United States includes 573 federally recognized American Indian and Alaska Native nations, of which the vast majority live in the U.S. West, including Alaska. What are now the states of Michigan and Wisconsin are home to the largest number of fedeally recognized American Indian tribes of any state east of the Mississippi River. Michigan includes 11 federally recognized Native nations, and Wisconsin includes 11 federally recognized tribal nations and one unrecognized tribal nation. Eight of the American Indian nations have historical roots in what is now Wisconsin that trace back centuries for some and thousands of years for others. Six of these eight tribal nations with deep roots are Anishinaabe. The Anishinaabe world is vast, spanning from the U.S. states of Michigan, Minnesota, North Dakota, and Wisconsin to the Canadian provinces of Ontario, Manitoba, and Saskatchewan. The Anishinaabe are culturally and linguistically related to one another, albeit with some variations in regional dialects and traditional practices. If counted as one group, the Anishinaabe would be one of the most populous American Indian groups of North America.

Northern Wisconsin is almost exclusively rural and White, with the exception of ten American Indian reservations, including the six Anishinaabe nations. Northwoods High School exists in one of the borderlands, near one of these reservations. Often, rural border towns near American Indian reservations are fraught with conflict, as White and Native American populations contest boundaries, land, natural resources, jobs, and other necessities. In border towns, Whites and Native Americans are more likely to interact and engage in all types of physical and cultural exchanges, with Native Americans often describing border towns as discriminating, biased, or prejudiced. Once holding title to the entire northern third of Wisconsin, the Anishinaabe people remaining in Wisconsin are now separated into six tribal nations, on six widely dispersed reservations of varying sizes within the state defined by treaties with the U.S. government. Holding onto a small chunk of their traditional lands, the participating tribal nation of Anishinaabe people have maintained the health of its forests, wildlife, and waterways through generations of tradition-based stewardship as relatives to the plant and animal communities that thrive there.

Although members of Wisconsin's 11 American Indian nations speak six different languages and have diverse cultural practices and diverse economic, political, and geographical landscapes, they are similar, like other American Indian communities, in disproportionately experiencing outcome

Figure 9.2. Precontact Territories of Various Early Tribes of Wisconsin Juxtaposed with Modern Reservations

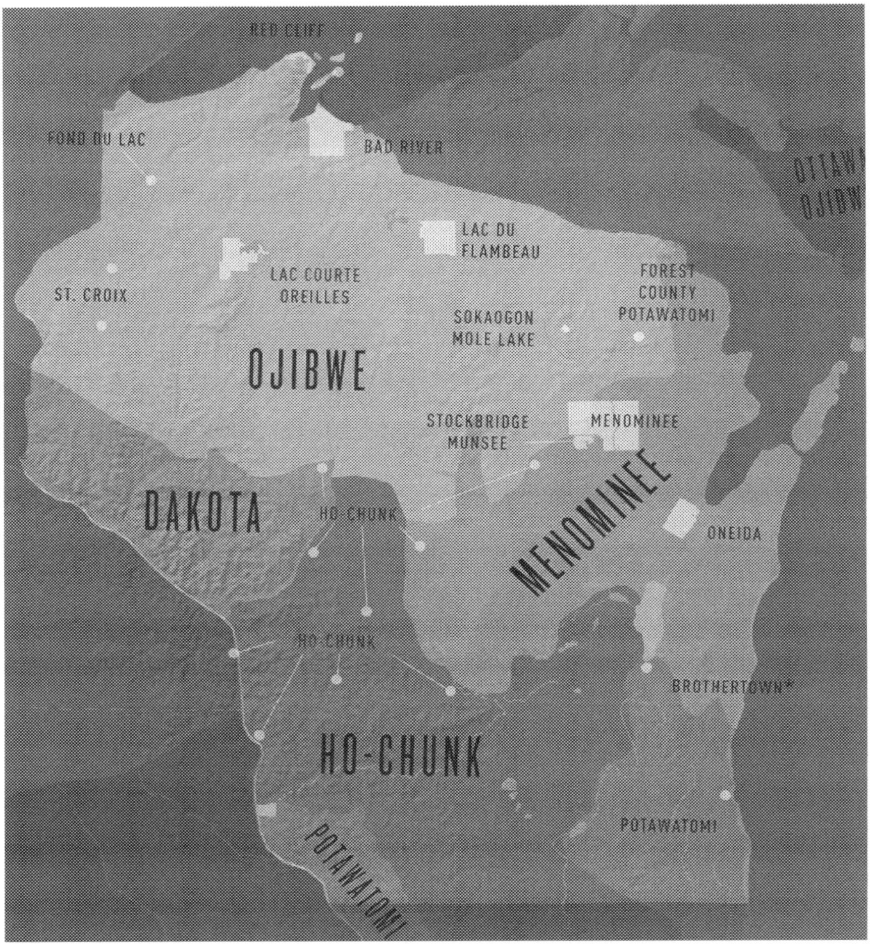

Note: The light gray area covering the northwest corner of Wisconsin indicates precontact Anishinaabe territory. The lightest gray areas delineate the current, federally recognized American Indian reservations of Wisconsin.

Source: Wisconsin First Nations Map Illustration from "The Ways" an educational resource from PBS Wisconsin. https://wisconsinfirstnations.org/map/

disparities in education and employment, living in poverty, and struggling with health, housing, and food security. Combined social and structural inequities, established by the white supremacist ideology under which the state was founded with the motto "Civilization Succeeds Barbarism," have generated behavioral outcome disparities for American Indian youth in Wisconsin. In a recent study, Bal, Betters-Bubon, and Fish (2019) analyzed all student- and school-level data in Wisconsin and found that American Indian students are two times more likely to receive exclusionary discipline compared to their White counterparts. American Indian students are three times more likely to be placed in special education programs and labeled as emotionally disturbed.

Historical Trauma of American Indian Nations

Since first contact with Europeans in the 1600s during the Fur Trade and Missionary eras, Native people of the Great Lakes were characterized by French explorers, traders, and missionaries as primitive savages, unpredictable and inconvenient obstacles to European colonization. American Indians who survived the Indian Wars and Indian Removal periods were subjected to assimilation in all areas of life. Boarding schools with little accountability and, later, public and parochial schools approached Indian education with the rod (to physically discipline) and the scissors (to cut hair in an effort to civilize), using both physical and psychological violence against American Indian children and youth for almost 100 years. An increased understanding today of the impacts of adverse childhood experiences illuminates the depth of trauma Indigenous youth experienced for a century.

Historically, the U.S. government described the presence of American Indians as the "Indian problem" (Brown, 1930). With their ancestors surviving disease, genocide, relocation, cultural loss, and loss of family, many American Indian children born near the start of the 20th century were forced to attend boarding schools like the infamous Carlisle Boarding School founded by Captain Richard H. Pratt. In 1892, Captain Pratt delivered a speech entitled "Kill the Indian, and Save the Man." This motto encapsulated additional federal and state policies like the Dawes Act of 1887, which carved up communally occupied Indigenous lands into individual parcels, forcing American Indians to adopt the individualistic American way of life versus the extended kinship of the tribal life led by their ancestors. The Bureau of Indian Affairs was initially created in the War Department, and U.S. federal Indian policy initially relegated Indigenous people to the jurisdiction of the U.S. Army, which frequently violated treaties and massacred, murdered, and removed countless people from their homelands.

The U.S. government's promotion of a settler-colonialist policy of genocide, forced migration, and assimilation through boarding schools and other means has created what Duran and Duran (1995) describe as a "soul wound." Acknowledging the presence of these longstanding effects of so much loss within Indigenous people helps inform understanding of their present circumstances. Such downward assimilationist practices in education began with the widespread use of boarding schools that separated

American Indian children from their families and communities, cut their hair, forbid them to speak their native languages or practice traditional customs, and forced them to learn English and practice Christianity, leading to cultural and spiritual genocide that current generations still carry. The boarding schools' systematic attempts to erase American Indian language and culture and to replace them with European American lifeways help explain the widespread destruction of Indigenous languages that contemporary tribal members are fighting to reverse today.

With the forced internment of Native Americans on reservations, fully 92% of Native Americans lived on reservations in 1950. Today, only 25% of Native Americans live on reservations due to various attempts to detribalize American Indian nations during the Termination era from the 1940s to the 1960s. Reservation life offered and continues to offer an opportunity for Indigenous nations to function as unified communities, although it often means not living on or near their ancestral lands. However, the Anishinaabe nation with which we collaborated in this project, like other Wisconsin Anishinaabe nations, is fortunate in that their current reservation boundaries include a small part of Anishinaabe ancestral territory, and tribal members still traditionally harvest wild rice, walleye, and musky fish from lakes, sometimes at night, by torchlight, in the traditional way that has been practiced for time immemorial in Northern Wisconsin.

The formal dissolution of assimilative boarding schools occurred with passage of the 1975 Indian Self-Determination and Educational Assistance Act. Urban American Indians and reservation American Indians without tribally run or federally run schools of their own were forced to attend local public schools, which remain legally responsible to educate all citizens, regardless of race or ethnic background. The 1975 Act helped hundreds of Native American nations establish their own tribally run schools, with oversight from the Bureau of Indian Affairs and the Bureau of Indian Education, now both located in the Department of the Interior. Though tribally run schools reserve the right to practice traditional culture, speak and teach the Indigenous language, and create curricula aligned with Indigenous worldviews and politics, school funding is usually tied to compliance with state standards, teacher licensing requirements, and other rules shared with institutions of public education.

In this study's context, most American Indian children first attend a public school on a reservation that serves grades K–8 with an almost exclusively American Indian student population. The Anishinaabe culture and language have always served and continue to serve as the powerful unifying theme of the school, which boasts colorful, bright student-created murals on walls that hold students' aspirations to a brighter future. However, American Indian youth are faced with challenges, dilemmas, trauma, and the compounded effects of poverty, high rates of substance abuse due to opioid epidemics, incarceration, and unemployment. Indigenous students are often defined by *what they are not*, as compared to middle-class suburban White youth who have historically formed the norm groups on standardized tests, IQ tests, and other measures of intelligence and academic achievement. When measured against culturally biased norms, American Indian students have historically underachieved in school indicators such as graduation rate, attendance, college admission test scores, and college attendance and graduation. These challenges have persisted for decades, as demonstrated in a 1966 State of Wisconsin Governor's Commission on Human Rights report on American Indian education:

> The state departments most closely concerned, the Department of Public Instruction and the Division of Children and Youth in the Department of Public Welfare, have emphasized a continuing and realistic effort to develop better understanding of the Indian student and his problems. This takes into account not only his need for better clothing and a quiet room in which to study, but also the fact that he is torn between two cultures. He is a part of both his environments, his home and his school. If his teachers can understand the great gulf that he must bridge when he faces the middle class, suburban-oriented school system and at the same time see the worth in his Indian heritage, then the chances are better that he will complete his education. (p. 51)

The City of Northwoods: Battlefield of the Walleye War

The city of Northwoods where the participating school is located was the epicenter of Wisconsin's anti-Indian movement of the 1980s and 1990s, which sprang from a fundamental misunderstanding of treaties and treaty rights by the non-Indigenous population of Wisconsin. During this time, racism and prejudice affected all aspects of life for the Anishinaabe, taking many forms, including attacks on traditional ways of life passed down from time immemorial. Panic narratives circulated in the Northwoods, condemning the local Anishinaabe nation's fish harvesting practices on public lands as illegal and leading to the destruction of fish populations. Conflicts over land and rights to hunt and fish helped fuel a widespread conflict from 1987 to 1991, during which tribal members were physically attacked or physically prevented from practicing their fishing rights on public lands ceded in treaties with the United States government (Nesper, 2002). Only a generation ago, tribal members risked injury as they encountered angry White protesters who gathered at boat landings as they fished, meeting hostile crowds of local White men, women, and children who threw rocks and other objects and held signs that said, "Spear an Indian! Save a Walleye," "Spear a Pregnant Squaw. Save Two Walleye", and "Timber N****R Go Back to the Reservation." An Indigenous Learning Lab member and a Northwoods High School alum, Jeremiah Lefebvre, remembers seeing his high school teachers at the boat landings, shouting and throwing objects at him and his family on the weekend, and then having to face the same teachers on Monday morning.

Northwoods High School: Learning in the Epicenter of the Anti-Indian Movement

Northwoods High serves as the only high school choice for Anishinaabe youth living on the reservation in this study. The large high school is 15 miles from the reservation. For the vast majority of the Anishinaabe youth, 9th grade is the first time they will attend school with others who don't share their culture, where four out of five students are non-Indigenous. Northwoods High School's student body comes from five public feeder schools, only one of which includes a substantial population of American Indian youth. Other feeder schools enroll almost exclusively White students from varying economic backgrounds.

Northwoods High School data from the last decade reveal conspicuous disparities in academic achievement, school dropout, and exclusionary discipline between American Indian and White students. For example, in 2015, although the Native American population at Northwoods was 21.3%, Native American students received over 60% of the suspensions and 100% of the expulsions (U.S. Department of Education, 2015). According to the Wisconsin Department of Public Instruction's 2019 School Report Card for Northwoods High, 80.8% of American Indian students scored Basic or Below Basic in English Language Arts Supplemental Data, as compared to 48.9% of White students. Math Supplemental Data reveal even larger racialized achievement gaps, with 93.9% of American Indian students scoring Basic or Below Basic, compared to 55.7% of White students. Since data have been collected, American Indian students attending Northwoods High have shown much lower graduation rates, lower standardized test scores and academic achievement on the ACT, and much higher rates of exclusionary discipline. This longstanding pattern of American Indian underachievement across school domains, coupled with the glaring racial disparity in exclusionary school discipline, is widely reflected across the United States for American Indian youth (U.S. Department of Education Office of Civil Rights, 2018).

The principal of the school explained the socioeconomic diversity starkly: "Some of our students come from four-million-dollar homes on a lake, and others slept in the Walmart parking lot last night" (Learning Lab #3). A majority of American Indian students at Northwoods High come from low-income families. From the beginning of their first year, Anishinaabe youth face many challenges as they try to relate to peers who are from the dominant White culture. Although many of their K–8 teachers at their reservation public school were White, the public school on the reservation embraces Anishinaabe culture and integrates it to teach curricular content. It strives to create a home-like atmosphere that encourages Anishinaabe identity and resilience. For most Anishinaabe first-year students at Northwoods High, their first school day is the first day they have been placed in direct competition and comparison with majority White peers. Anishinaabe youth are not the only ones struggling with this demographic reality—Northwoods High staff have been forced to adjust their school practices with the influx of American Indian youth from the reservation.

Over the past decade, administrators and teachers tried various ways of mitigating the conflicts between White and American Indian youth, of increasing academic performance of Native students, of restoring relationships with the Anishinaabe community, and of incorporating Anishinaabe cultural practices. As a direct result of the Walleye War, Wisconsin passed Act 31 in 1989, which included state statutes requiring that "[A]ll public school districts and pre-service education programs provide instruction on the history, culture, and tribal sovereignty of Wisconsin's eleven federally-recognized American Indian nations and tribal communities" (Wisconsin Department of Public Instruction, n.d., para.1). Northwoods High complies with Act 31 by offering three courses in American Indian Studies: American Indian History, American Indian Literature, and Anishinaabe Language and Culture I & II. Currently, two American Indian counselors help Anishinaabe youth navigate the academic and social demands of Northwoods High and guide administrators and teachers in incorporating Anishinaabe culture within their behavioral and academic curricula.

Recent efforts in 2017 made school history when an eagle staff was presented to Northwoods High from the Anishinaabe nation, as a symbol of good faith and trust. Eagle staffs are symbols of Native American communities, created from eagle feathers under strict cultural protocols. The gifting of an eagle staff to Northwoods High was significant, a harbinger of encouragement, trust-building, and healing. The Thunderbird has been the mascot of Northwoods High for generations, albeit the mascot has not been recently viewed or understood by White school staff as an Indigenous cultural teaching and is mostly referred to as "T-Bird," as school staff associate it with European and European American traditions. Thunderbird stories exist in many Indigenous cultures of North America, including the Anishinaabe. Although the school has not yet fully examined the Thunderbird mascot from an Indigenous lens, this Anishinaabe cultural symbol connects the institution with the unique place of the school and connects the institution to a powerful symbol of spiritual healing and renewal for Anishinaabe people. These recent, positive systemic efforts and the willingness and commitment of Northwoods High leadership were important factors for the research team to select Northwoods High School as the intervention site.

INDIGENOUS LEARNING LAB PROJECT

The culturally responsive positive behavior interventions and supports (CRPBIS) team has built a reciprocal partnership with multiple local school communities to facilitate collective agency among school community members and create ecologically valid, sustainable systemic solutions to racial disproportionality in behavioral outcomes. In addition, the project has built capacity for inclusive knowledge production and decisionmaking in local schools, districts, and the state's education agency (Bal, 2016; 2018; Bal et al., 2018; Bal, Afacan, & Cakir, 2019). Indigenous Learning Lab is a methodological scale-up through a strategic combination of processes and tools for systemic change in organizations facing enduring and disabling systemic crises. Decolonizing and critical Indigenous scholarship generates emancipatory solutions that address the unique needs of American Indian youth while at the same time they promote a positive, supportive, effective, and adaptive school climate for *all* students and adults in schools.

Cultural and linguistic revitalization, validation of indigenous epistemology and knowledge systems, and exercising educational self-sovereignty are critical components of designing a culturally decolonizing system of support (Brayboy, 2006; Castagno & Brayboy, 2008; Lomawaima & McCarty, 2006). Utilizing a critical lens informed by interdisciplinary literature including decolonizing methodology (Smith, 2012; Tuck & Yang, 2014), critical Indigenous pedagogies (Brayboy, 2006; Grande, 2004; McCarty & Lee, 2014), Positive Behavior Interventions and Supports (PBIS) scholarship (Sugai & Horner, 2006), and cultural-historical activity theory and formative intervention research (Engeström, 2016), the Indigenous Learning Lab project aims to leverage ingenuity, resilience, funds of knowledge, and epistemologies of the local tribal community. Learning Lab takes coalition-building, refusal of damage-centered epistemology, and design-based implementation from the ground up as architectural foundations that address racialized behavioral outcome disparities (see Figure 9.3).

Building Strategic Coalitions for Systemic Transformation

Building a reciprocal partnership with the Northwoods High School and district leadership, the local Anishinaabe tribe, the Wisconsin Indian Education Association (WIEA), the Wisconsin Department of Public Instruction (WDPI), and the state's Disproportionality Technical Assistance Network traces back to 2017. Before starting the intervention, we spent two years in the field to build this strategic, equity-oriented coalition. Our research team visited several schools in Wisconsin serving American Indian nations.

Figure 9.3. Blueprint of the Indigenous Learning Lab Project

Collaborative Design of New Behavioral Support System (2019–2020 school year)

Implementation of New Behavioral Support System (2020–2021 academic year)

Sustained Improvement (2021–2022 academic year)

- CLOSE the disciplinary gap
- PROMOTE positive school climate and safety
- CREATE culturally responsive learning environment

Researcher–Practitioners–Families–Community Partnership: Culturally Responsive Partnership-Building	Refusal of Damage-Centered Epistemology Toward Desires for Indigenous Prolepsis	Design-Based Implementation from Ground Up

In 2017, Northwoods High School attained laudable achievement in closing the graduation gap between White students and American Indian students. However, the gaps in academic achievement and disciplinary actions continued to hinder school administrators' transformative effort to better serve all students. The former principal and American Indian mentors recognized that the school community still suffers from intergenerational trauma stemming from historically accumulated disturbances and ruptures (e.g., the Walleye War).

While identifying the site, the CRPBIS research team added new members. A Native American scholar and the then-assistant dean of student diversity programs in the school of education at the University of Wisconsin–Madison, Aaron Bird Bear (Mandan, Hidatsa, and Diné Nations), joined the team as a co-principal investigator. In addition, we recruited an American Indian graduate student and former science teacher, Linda Orie (Oneida Nation of Wisconsin), as a Project Assistant. The research team is led by Aaron Bird Bear and special education professor Aydin Bal, who developed the Learning Lab methodology and facilitated prior Learning Labs. We also formed an advisory board including Indigenous scholars and leaders: Ned Blackhawk, a professor of history at Yale University (Western Shoshone); Brian Jackson (Anishinaabe) of WIEA; David O'Connor (Bad River) of WDPI; Sage Birdsbill (Anishinaabe), a high school student; Gloria Ladson-Billings at the University of Wisconsin and National Academy of Education; Alfredo Artiles at Stanford University; and Annalisa Sannino at the University of Tampere, Finland. The CRPBIS team continued to expand partnership with multiple agencies. We reached out to American Indian scholars and students at the University of Wisconsin–Madison and the university outreach specialists, who have had extensive working experiences with Native American communities.

In the Upper Great Lakes Region culture, offering tobacco to tribal partners is a traditional way to build relationships based on trust and integrity. At that time, the Department of Life Sciences Communication at the University of Wisconsin launched a ceremonial tobacco-growing project revitalizing seeds indigenous to North America. Aaron Bird Bear suggested the use of traditional ceremonial tobacco as a means for building culturally responsive partnering. The CRPBIS team obtained harvested tobacco. As we visited multiple American Indian communities for site identification, we presented tobacco to the community leaders. In the 2019 Fall semester, we started Indigenous Learning Lab. We held the first two meetings at the Anishinaabe reservation community center. We offered child care, food, and transportation to all participating members. We started each session with a pipe and smudging ceremony by burning traditional tobacco and sage. Jeremiah Lefebvre, the American Indian school counselor, serves as the project liaison along with Kevin Burt, the principal of the school, and Lola Johnson, an Anishinaabe community member working as an administrator in her tribal nation's department of education. Mr. Lefebvre led the opening pipe and smudging ceremonies as a starting ritual to fill the meeting space with positivity and dispel negative energy such as mistrust, conflicts, and confrontations between Native American and non-Native American members (see Figure 9.4).

Figure 9.4. Mr. Lefebvre's Supplies for Pipe and Smudging Ceremonies

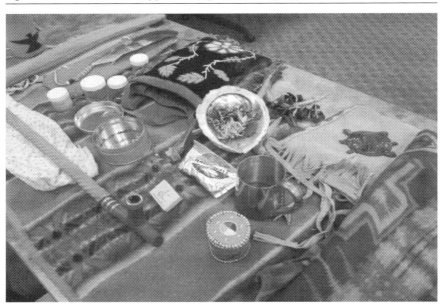

Photo credit: Aydin Bal

While the CRPBIS team began building a partnership with Northwoods High's school community, we experienced a change in the school leadership team. The new school principal, who had been serving as an assistant principal of the school, committed to the project. The CRPBIS team collaboratively worked with the community and school liaisons to hold first and second Indigenous Learning Lab meetings on the reservation to disrupt asymmetrical power relations embedded in the bureaucratic school system. The community liaison suggested using the tribal education department building as a meeting place where Anishinaabe parents and tribal community members can easily participate in meetings. Anishinaabe members supported Learning Lab meetings by providing meals that utilized harvested wild rice. In this local Anishinaabe band, like all others, wild rice (*manoomin*) is considered a sacred food that symbolizes the spiritual connection to the land and is served at tribal ceremonies (Vennum, 1988). The CRPBIS team collaboratively develops meeting agendas for each session (e.g., meeting flows, meal plan, participant recruitment) to empower local educators to lead systemic transformation process.

As suggested by the Anishinaabe community members, the research team introduced the Seven Grandfather Teachings of the Anishinaabe as inclusive group norms to run a mutually respectful problem-solving process. In Anishinaabe, the Seven Grandfather Teachings are orally passed down moral and ethical principles that elders have used to educate future generations on living a good life:

- Nibwaakaawin (Wisdom)
- Zaagi'idiwin (Love)
- Minaadendamowin (Respect)
- Aakode'ewin (Bravery)
- Gwayakwaadiziwin (Honesty)
- Dabaadendiziwin (Humility)
- Debwewin (Truth)

Indigenous Learning Lab members jointly adopted Respect, Love, Honesty, Truth, Bravery, and Humility to develop collective problem identification and problem-solving Wisdom. Members particularly emphasized Bravery to stand up to obdurate injustice such as racial disproportionality with integrity, convictions, and courage to develop "politized trust"—"establishing trust with community partners, especially in communities that serve students from nondominant groups, requires not only a personal working relationship but also a political or racial solidarity" (Vakil et al., 2016, p. 199).

Through Indigenous Learning Lab, for the first time in Northwoods High School's history, the school leaders asked American Indian students and community members to join them in creating a new, schoolwide, equitable, effective, and culturally responsive behavior support system. Principal Burt and staff participating in this research project exhibit many of the Seven Grandfather Teachings that guide traditional Anishinaabe values. For example, the school leadership demonstrated wisdom, humility, and honesty by admitting room for growth in discipline and academic achievement and acknowledging the large opportunity and achievement gap between White and Anishinaabe students that has plagued the school from the beginning. As members engaged in questioning in the first meetings, the principal demonstrated genuine commitment to disrupt not only the discipline disproportionality but also academic disparities.

The leadership did not deny the existence of a real problem, but instead was open to the risky idea that perhaps the very school systems established and used for decades are partially to blame for the patterns of racialized conflict and underachievement of tribal youth. The administrators and staff who have committed to participating in this difficult boundary-crossing, distributed leadership, and collective agency work should be recognized for their Bravery, as the outcomes are uncertain as this type of innovation has not been tried before and requires power-sharing with Anishinaabe parents, community members, and students. See Figure 9.5 for an Indigenous Learning Lab session focused on analyzing and modeling.

Figure 9.5. Indigenous Learning Lab Members Engaged in Analyzing and Modeling

Refusal of Damage-Centered Epistemology Toward Desire for Indigenous Prolepsis

Indigenous Learning Lab builds upon "refusal" of metanarrative in social science research and leverages "resistance, reclaiming, recovery, reciprocity, repatriation, [and] regeneration" (Tuck & Yang, 2014, p. 244) as a transformative tool to fight against damage-centered epistemology. We adapted Michael Cole's (1996) creative appropriation of the notion of *prolepsis* as "the cultural mechanism that brings the end into the beginning" (p. 183), meaning "the representation of a future act or development as being presently existing" (p. 239). Humans are social in a sense that is different from the sociability of other species. Only a culture-using human being can "reach into" the cultural past, project it into the future, and then "carry" that conceptual future "back" into the present to create the sociocultural environment of the newcomer" (Cole, 2007, p. 240). Indigenous Learning Lab redirected researchers' and school leaders' gaze toward *Indigenous prolepsis* to foster collaborative agency and vision of possible futures, and to produce locally meaningful solutions developed by Indigenous community members.

Indigenous Learning Lab pursues an epistemological and axiological shift from settler-colonial knowledge production activity within the metanarrative of social science research that tries to find damages or pains (e.g., hypervisibility in mental health problems, disability identification) and then develops and implements remedial interventions to fix the perceived deficits (Tuck, 2009). We acknowledge painful narratives indexed in critical histories of American Indian communities in a settler colonial societal structure that generates structural inequities and intergenerational traumas, unresolved grief, and materialized outcome disparities in health, education, housing, the justice system, and employment. The Indigenous Learning Lab project aims to contribute to an epistemological shift by tapping into cultural wealth, spirituality, and traditional healing strategies that counteract negative, cumulative impacts of the legacy of settler colonization and the more recent anti-Indian movement.

Indigenous Learning Lab sessions aim to promote proleptic design through the exercise of stakeholders' agency as:

> a temporally embedded process of social engagement, informed by the past (in its habitual aspect), but also oriented toward the future (as a capacity to imagine alternative possibilities) and toward the present (as a capacity to contextualize past habits and future projects within the contingencies of the moment). (Emirbayer & Mische, 1998, p. 963)

Figure 9.6. Indigenous Prolepsis in Collaborative Design Endeavor for Future-Making

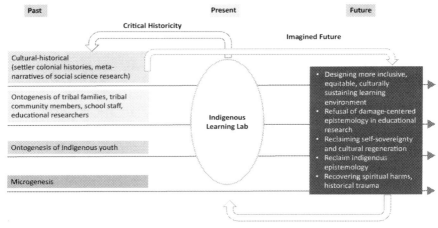

Figure 9.6 shows the design features of Indigenous Learning Lab. In this representation, we expanded Michael Cole's (2007) conceptualization of individual development in multiple time scales to historicize the collective work of Learning Lab members. We used Cole's three time scales: cultural-historical (history of cultural groups), ontogenetic (history of individuals), and microgenetic (moment-to-moment interactions of individuals). As the figure indicates, members engage in epistemic inquiry into critical colonial historicity engraved in everyday institutional and instructional practices, and school–community relationships. They bring historicity to interpret and analyze stubborn educational conundrums in the present, such as racial disparities, then collectively envision a more equitable future learning ecology.

Design-Based Implementation from the Ground Up

The guiding principles of Indigenous Learning Lab (*respect, revitalization,* and *reconciliation)* constitute transformative desires toward Indigenous prolepsis by dismantling the settler colonial system in a public school and reclaiming tribal sovereignty for the future of education systems. Indigenous Learning Lab pursues a paradigm shift in education research, moving from the "knowledge transfer metaphor" embedded in traditional experimental research in which researchers develop decontextualized and universally applicable solutions, and practitioners implement solutions with integrity (Ko & Bal, 2019; Penuel, 2014).

Local educational sites are filled with diverging interpretations, resistance, and competing priorities (Engeström, 2011). To address complex and localized inequity in education, contextually situated systemic design and transformation efforts are required to develop locally meaningful and adaptive solutions in responsive to ever-changing local dynamics (Artiles, 2019; Bal, 2017; Gutiérrez & Penuel, 2014). Empowering local stakeholders to lead transformative systemic change through design-based implementation from the ground up, Indigenous Learning Lab facilitates contextual responsiveness to specific social-historical-spatial contexts.

Formative expansion of Indigenous Learning Lab membership. The CRPBIS team worked with school and community liaisons to recruit potential members who have rich expertise and experiences related to school discipline and community-school relationships. Initially, Indigenous Learning Lab held its first meeting with eight local stakeholders (principal, assistant principal, social worker, two community members, one American Indian education mentor, one student, and one parent). As meetings proceeded, members were encouraged to identify whose voices should also be included in the Lab. In the first meeting, members suggested having more voices of classroom teachers and students who witness or engage in daily behavioral incidents. Also, members wanted to learn about the transition experience of American Indian youth from the K–8 public school on the reservation to Northwoods High School. Members decided to invite an American Indian teacher from the school on the reservation. It was also suggested to include the director of special education at Northwoods. Members exercised their transformative agency in the recruitment process beyond the given frame of dominant participation structure in educational research practice in which researchers select and recruit participants. Each participant was given the right to select their pseudonym. Table 9.1 exhibits the final composition of Indigenous Learning Lab.

Interactive design and implementation. Indigenous Learning Lab includes three phases: (1) designing a culturally decolonizing behavioral support system, (2) implementing this new system of support, and (3) sustainably improving and institutionalizing the culturally responsive system of support. In the CRPBIS Project, there have been five previous Learning Labs formed at two elementary schools, two middle schools, and one high school in two school districts (Bal, 2018). In the previous Labs, the research team worked with the schools to facilitate only the *design* of culturally responsive behavioral support systems. In Indigenous Learning Lab, we are working with the school during the implementation and sustainability phases of the new system.

Table 9.2 includes the main agenda of each Indigenous Learning Lab session. As an inclusive knowledge production activity to unite competing motives and goals among stakeholders, Indigenous Learning Lab takes the historically accumulated conflicts within a school community as a developmental opportunity to transform the existing system. In addition to forming an inclusive problem-solving group, the CRPBIS team worked with school administrators to prepare multiple mirroring data that galvanizes critical praxis of Learning Lab members—"reflection and action upon the world in order to transform it" (Freire, 2000, p. 51).

Table 9.1. Demographic Information of Participants

Participant Name*		Roles	Race	Gender
Kevin	School administrators	Principal	White	Male
Bart		Assistant principal & dean of student affairs	White	Male
Gwenwyn		Director of special education	White	Female
Jeremiah	Educators & staff	American Indian education mentor	Native American	Male
Carson		Social worker/ student support strategist	White	Male
Susan		Classroom teacher	White	Male
Jane		Classroom teacher	White	Female
Kate		K–8 public school classroom teacher	Native American	Female
Lola	Parents & community members	Vocational/higher education transition coordinator of the tribal education department	Native American	Female
Diana		Community member	Native American	Female
Black		Parent, community member	Native American	Male
Matthew	Students	Current student	Native American	Male
Darren		Current student	Native American	Male
Ada		Current student	White	Female

*Pseudonyms are used to conceal identity of the participants. Participants selected their own pseudonyms.

At the first meeting, the principal presented the academic and behavioral outcome data to promote the systemic diagnosis of Northwoods High School's present state. Historically accumulated and ongoing racialized outcome disparities were invisible in those seemingly neutral statistical data. During the first meeting, tribal members criticized the limitation of school-level aggregated data in representing the experience of Anishinaabe youth at Northwoods High School. They requested academic

Table 9.2. Tentative Agendas of Indigenous Learning Lab Sessions

Sessions	Date	Purpose of the Session
Learning Lab #1	10/2019	Introducing the project and data-sharing
Learning Lab #2	11/2019	Describing Learning Lab activity and sharing expectations and goals
Learning Lab #3	12/2019	Focusing on membership and disproportionality data
Learning Lab #4	01/2020	Reviewing disciplinary data and disproportionality discussion
Learning Lab #5	02/2020	Mapping out existing discipline system (1)
Learning Lab #6	03/2020	Mapping out and expanding the existing system (2)
Learning Lab #7	04/2020	Creating and developing a culturally responsive schoolwide behavior support system
Learning Lab #8	05/2020	Refining and finalizing the new behavior support system
Learning Lab #9	06/2020	Reviewing and reflecting on the new system and the Learning Lab process

and behavioral outcome data be disaggregated by students' race to better understand the extent of systemic inequities. In response to the request, the research team and administrators together reanalyzed and visualized complex school outcome data. Disaggregated outcome data were used as a reflective tool in the next meeting to help members critically interrogate the school's outcome data. Members engaged in collectively mapping out systemic acts and processes that generate outcome disparities and modeling the new system. They have successfully completed the design phase and developed the new culturally responsive behavioral support system that is more just, student-centered, and sustainable in the eyes of school staff and Anishinaabe students and parents. Currently, the school and our research team are moving into the second phase, implementation of the new system in the 2020–2021 academic year. The newly designed support system is not a fixed entity. Instead, it is a living, adaptive artifact in response to ever-shifting local dynamics. The implementation team at Northwoods is working on realigning the new support system to mitigate collateral damages of the COVID-19 pandemic (e.g., addressing increased truancy by bolstering student-teacher relationships).

CONCLUSION

Starting the second decade of the 21st century, humanity is facing a global crisis, the COVID-19 pandemic. Under such extreme and elusive circumstances, the community-led, transformational, and collective-agency-oriented design of Indigenous Learning Lab has given our team an important advantage. Global crises are a natural outcome of global capitalism and will be a part of our near future (Bal, 2017). Formative interventionists are responsive to the ever-changing possibilities and constrains of local contexts. Yrjö Engeström (2013) stated the theoretical positions of formative interventions in education, public health, and other fields:

> The world seems more out of control than ever. Often the very striving for complete control, or absolutistic thinking to use the terminology of John Dewey, plays a central part behind personal failures . . . The implication is that instead of controlling the world, we should accept that all our designs have unintended consequences and drift in unexpected ways. Thus, instead of pushing the grand designs through at any costs, we might cultivate tentative solutions by means of experimentation, first locally and, when working solutions are found, by generalizing and spreading them through dialogue and further experimentations. (p. xv)

Racial disproportionality in school discipline is a persistent, complex systemic problem. It demands persistent, complex systemic solutions developed and tested in practice by local stakeholders, especially those who have been historically excluded from knowledge production and decision-making activities in education (Bal, 2018). In the Indigenous Learning Lab project, we conceptualize cultural responsiveness as an inclusive systemic design process—Learning Lab, through which local stakeholders develop their own culturally responsive schoolwide system of behavioral support. The new system includes a new object (all students and adults in the school community) and an expanded systemic structure organized around the new object (expanded rules, roles, division of labor, tools, and community) for the creation of positive, inclusive, and expansive school culture and climate. The new system is conceptualized as a living artifact that is open to change based on the ever-changing needs, strengths, and goals of their local school community and larger sociopolitical context. Collaborative collection and analysis of multiple forms of the dataset (e.g., discipline data, school climate survey results, interviews with stakeholders), collected through the implementation phase, will be used during the interactive, iterative redesign of the behavioral support model to ensure sustained improvement and local institutionalization of new solutions.

The United States was founded on settler colonialism, capitalism, and slavery. American Indian youth have experienced a hostile schooling system that invalidates sovereignty and self-determination of tribal nations (Brayboy, 2006; Tuck, 2009). A ripple effect of the long history of criminalization of cultures and languages and downward assimilation continually impacts American Indian youth's everyday educational experiences deployed through an oppressive form of pedagogical, institutional, and interactional practices (Sabzalian, 2019; San Pedro, 2014). To offset the cumulative effects of historical and ongoing settler-colonial harms, critical Indigenous scholarship has emphasized the necessity of building culturally decolonizing education systems (Brayboy, 2006; Grande, 2004; McCarty & Lee, 2014). Informed by intersectionality, decolonizing epistemologies, and a theory of organizational change (Engeström, 1987; 2011), Indigenous Learning Lab took a "morally engaged research/researcher approach" (King, 2017) to create equity-oriented systems of support through epistemological and axiological innovations. Learning Lab draws on critical historicity, participatory justice, and equity as guiding principles. This collective systemic design process was utilized to generate ecologically valid solutions to address racial disproportionality in school discipline and special education identification (e.g., behavioral disorders) and postcapitalist and colonialist inclusive future-making through a strategic university-school-family-community partnership for building a socially just school system for *all*.

REFERENCES

Artiles, A. J. (2011). Toward an interdisciplinary understanding of educational equity and difference: The case of the racialization of ability. *Educational Researcher, 40*(9), 431–445.

Artiles, A. J. (2019). Reenvisioning equity research: Disability identification disparities as a case in point. *Educational Researcher, 48*(6), 325–335.

Bal, A. (2011). *Culturally responsive school-wide positive behavioral interventions and supports framework*. Wisconsin Department of Public Instruction.

Bal, A. (2012). Participatory social justice for all. In L. G. Denti & P. A. Whang (Eds.), *Rattling chains: Exploring social justice in education* (pp. 99–110). Boston, MA: Sense.

Bal, A. (2016). From intervention to innovation: A cultural-historical approach to the racialization of school discipline. *Interchange, 47*(4), 409–427. https://doi.org/10.1007/s10780-016-9280-z

Bal, A. (2017). System of disability. *Critical Education, 8*(6), 1–27.

Bal, A. (2018). Culturally responsive positive behavioral interventions and supports: A process-oriented framework for systemic transformation. *Review of Education, Pedagogy, and Cultural Studies, 40*(2), 144–174.

Bal, A., Afacan, K., & Cakir, H. I. (2018). Culturally responsive school discipline: Implementing learning lab at a high school for systemic transformation. *American Educational Research Journal, 55*(5), 1007–1050.

Bal, A., Afacan, K., & Cakir, H. (2019). Transforming schools from the ground-up with local stakeholders: Implementing Learning Lab for inclusion and systemic transformation at a middle school. *Interchange: A Quarterly Review of Education, 50*(3), 359–387.

Bal, A., Betters-Bubon, J., & Fish, R. E. (2019). A multilevel analysis of statewide disproportionality in exclusionary discipline and the identification of emotional disturbance. *Education and Urban Society, 51*(2), 247–268.

Brayboy, B. M. J. (2006). Toward a tribal critical race theory in education. *The Urban Review, 37*(5), 425–446.

Brown, R. A. (1930). The Indian problem and the law. *The Yale Law Journal, 39*(3), 307–331.

Castagno, A. E., & Brayboy, B. M. J. (2008). Culturally responsive schooling for indigenous youth: A review of the literature. *Review of Educational Research, 78*(4), 941–993. https://doi.org/10.3102/0034654308323036

Carter, P. L., Skiba, R., Arredondo, M. I., & Pollock, M. (2016). You can't fix what you don't look at: Acknowledging race in addressing racial discipline disparities. *Urban Education, 52*(2), 207–235. https://doi.org/10.1177/0042085916660350

Cavendish, W., Artiles, A., & Harry, B. (2014). Tracking inequality 60 years after *Brown*: Does policy legitimize the racialization of disability? *Multiple Voices for Ethnically Diverse Exceptional Learners, 14*(2), 30–40.

Cole, M. (1996). *Cultural Psychology*. Harvard University Press.

Cole, M. (2007). Phylogeny and cultural history in ontogeny. *Journal of Physiology Paris, 101*, 236–246.

Crenshaw, K. (1991). Mapping the margins: Intersectionality, identity politics, and violence against women of color. *Stanford Law Review, 43*(6), 1241–1299.

Duran, E., & Duran, B. (1995). *Native American postcolonial psychology*. State University of New York Press.

Emirbayer, M., & Mische, A. (1998). What is agency? *American Journal of Sociology, 103*(4), 962–1023.

Engeström, Y. (1987). *Learning by expanding: An activity-theoretical approach to developmental research*. Orienta-Konsultit.

Engeström, Y. (2011). From design experiments to formative interventions. *Theory & Psychology, 21*(5), 598–628.

Engeström, Y. (2013). Forward: Formative interventions for expansive learning. In J. Virkkunen & D. S. Newnham, *The Change Laboratory: A tool for collaborative development of work and education* (pp. xv–xx). Sense.

Engeström, Y. (2016). *Studies in expansive learning: Learning what is not yet there*. Cambridge University Press.

Engeström, Y., & Sannino, A. (2010). Studies of expansive learning: Foundations, findings and future challenges. *Educational Research Review, 5*(1), 1–24.

Freire, P. (2000). *Pedagogy of the oppressed* (M. B. Ramos, Trans.). Bloomsbury.

Grande, S. (2004). *Red pedagogy*. Rowman and Littlefield.

Gregory, A., Skiba, R. J., & Noguera, P. A. (2010). The achievement gap and the discipline gap: Two sides of the same coin? *Educational Researcher, 39*(1), 59–68.

Gutiérrez, K. D., & Penuel, W. R. (2014). Relevance to practice as a criterion for rigor. *Educational Researcher, 43*(1), 19–23.

Kim, C., Losen, D., & Hewitt, D. (2010). *The school-to-prison pipeline: Structuring legal reform*. New York University Press.

King, J. E. (2017). Morally engaged research/ers: Dismantling epistemological nihilation in the age of impunity. *Educational Researcher, 46*(5), 211–222.

Ko, D., & Bal, A. (2019). Rhizomatic research design in a smooth space of learning: Rupturing, connecting and generating. *Critical Education, 10*(17), 1–20.

Lomawaima, K. T., & McCarty, T. L. (2006). *To remain an Indian: Lessons in democracy from a century of Native American education.* Teachers College Press.

Marx, K., & Engels, F. (2017). *The holy family.* Andesite Press. (Original work published 1884)

McCarty, T. L., & Lee, T. S. (2014). Critical culturally sustaining/revitalizing pedagogy and indigenous education sovereignty. *Harvard Educational Review, 84*(1), 101–124.

McInnes, B. D. (2019, April). *Future directions in indigenous education research.* Paper presented at the Wisconsin Center for Education Research, Madison, WI.

Morris, M. (2016). *Pushout: The criminalization of black girls in schools.* The New Press.

National Congress of American Indians. (2020). *Indian Country demographics.* http://www.ncai.org/about-tribes/demographics

Nesper, L. (2002). *The walleye war: The struggle for Ojibwe spearfishing and treaty rights.* University of Nebraska Press.

Orfield, G., Siegel-Hawley, G., & Kucsera, J. (2014). *Sorting out deepening confusion on segregation trends.* The Civil Rights Project.

Penuel, W. R. (2014). Emerging forms of formative intervention research in education. *Mind, Culture, and Activity, 21*(2), 97–117.

Roosevelt, T. (1901, December). *State of the Union.* http://www.let.rug.nl/usa/presidents/theodore-roosevelt/state-of-the-union-1901.php

Sabzalian, L. (2019). *Indigenous children's survivance in public schools.* Routledge.

San Pedro, T. J. (2014). Internal and environmental safety zones: Navigating expansions and contractions of identity between indigenous and colonial paradigms, pedagogies, and classrooms. *Journal of American Indian Education, 53*(3), 42–62.

Sannino, A., Engeström, Y., & Lemos, M. (2016). Formative interventions for expansive learning and transformative agency. *Journal of the Learning Sciences, 25*(4), 599–633.

Skiba, R. J., Michael, R. S., Nardo, A. C., & Peterson, R. L. (2002). The color of discipline: Sources of racial and gender disproportionality in school punishment. *The Urban Review, 34*(4), 317–342.

Skiba, R. J., Chung, C.-G., Trachok, M., Baker, T. L., Sheya, A., & Hughes, R. L. (2014). Parsing disciplinary disproportionality: Contributions of infraction, student, and school characteristics to out-of-school suspension and expulsion. *American Educational Research Journal, 51*(4), 640–670.

Smith, D. M. (2017, November). *Counting the dead: Estimating the loss of life in the Indigenous holocaust, 1492-present.* The paper presented at the 2017 Native American Symposium at Southern Oklahoma University, Durant, OK.

Smith, L. T. (2012). *Decolonizing methodologies: Research and indigenous peoples* (2nd ed.). Zed Books.

State of Wisconsin, Governor's Commission on Human Rights. (1966). *Handbook on Wisconsin Indians.* University of Wisconsin Extension.

Sugai, G., & Horner, R. R. (2006). A promising approach for expanding and sustaining school-wide positive behavior support. *School Psychology Review, 35*(2), 245–259.

Tuck, E. (2009). Suspending damage: A letter to communities. *Harvard Educational Review, 79*(3), 409–427.

Tuck, E., & Yang, K. W. (2014). R-words: Refusing research. In D. Paris & M. T. Winn (Eds.), *Humanizing research: Decolonizing qualitative inquiry with youth and communities* (pp. 223–248). Sage.

U.S. Department of Education, Office for Civil Rights. (2015). *Civil rights data collection.* https://ocrdata.ed.gov/

U.S. Department of Education, Office for Civil Rights. (2018, April 14). *Civil rights data collection.* https://ocrdata.ed.gov/

Vakil, S., McKinney de Royston, M., Suad Nasir, N., & Kirshner, B. (2016). Rethinking race and power in design-based research: Reflections from the field. *Cognition and Instruction, 34*(3), 194–209.

Vennum, T. (1988). *Wild rice and the Ojibway people.* Minnesota Historical Society Press.

Welsh, R. O., & Little, S. (2018). The school discipline dilemma: A comprehensive review of disparities and alternative approaches. *Review of Educational Research, 88*(5), 752–794.

Wisconsin Department of Public Instruction. (2019). *Accountability report cards.* https://apps2.dpi.wi.gov/reportcards

Wisconsin Department of Public Instruction. (n.d.). *State statutes for American Indian studies in Wisconsin.* https://dpi.wi.gov/amind/state-statues

Wolfe, P. (2006) Settler colonialism and the elimination of the native. *Journal of Genocide Research, 8*(4), 387–409.

Conclusion

Wendy Cavendish and Jennifer F. Samson

The equity-focused intent of education policy and research is often at odds with implementation and rarely centers the lived experiences of those most impacted. So although there exists an abundance of educational research, policies, and practices intended to promote greater equity across socially determined identities such as race, language, class, gender, and dis/ability (e.g., Annamma et al., 2013), many policy and research approaches treat socially determined identities as static, discrete subgroup labels applied to those being studied or politicized. We assert instead that race, language, class, gender, dis/ability, and citizenship are not discrete identity markers but rather must be considered as "reciprocally constructing phenomena that shape complex social inequalities" (Collins, 2015, p. 2). Additionally, there is often limited reflection on or reporting of who the researchers or policymakers are themselves, and minimal consideration of the often privileged positions from which they frame their work. This detachment from native understandings of equity issues yields policies and research that often fail to effect meaningful change for those situated at intersecting axes of identities subject to sociocultural disadvantage and oppression (Crenshaw, 1994; Collins, 2015; Hankivsky et al., 2014).

Drawing from Collins and Bilge's (2016) core components of relationality, power, and social inequality, we advocate for equity to be centered when intersectionality is applied to policy, practice, and research analyses. These notions of power and privilege are central to an understanding of intersectionality as an analytic lens and distinct from work that simply includes two or more identity markers and claims to be intersectional. There is great potential in the broader application of intersectionality to include the crossing of methodological (qualitative/quantitative), systemic (micro/macro), and positional (teacher, researcher, policymaker) barriers embedded within structures of power and privilege. The strength of an equity-based intersectionality framework is that it facilitates the recognition and examination of interactions in many domains (hegemonic, structural, interpersonal, individual) and so allows for a comprehensive view of policy impact (Hancock, 2007). This approach is critical for understanding multidimensional aspects of education policy development and implementation; specifically, how problems are defined and addressed, by whom, and how policy and research are evaluated (Hankivsky & Cormier, 2011).

In this book, our collective goal was to provide diverse and meaningful examples of ways to conceptualize and apply a framework for equity-focused intersectionality work in education and across disciplines. In particular, we hope that this book motivates readers to consider intersectionality in more explicit and applied ways that extend beyond theoretical considerations. Throughout the chapters, the application of guiding questions within the IBA framework challenges reproduction of inequities and power differentials within the discussed research and policymaking processes. The authors in this volume highlight ways in which dynamic processes can be examined to include the interactions among policy development and enactment, practices within educational settings, and research on educational settings. This approach, as used by chapter authors, demonstrates myriad ways policymakers, researchers, and practitioners can consider socially constructed identities and the interactions of such identity markers within enacted policy and research across multiple disciplines and social systems.

Specifically, in Section I, chapter authors center structural racism and provide cross-system and cross-disciplinary considerations that include macro and sociohistorical views of systems that interact with education, including civil rights law, disparate policing policies of Black and Brown bodies, and criminology theories related to discipline policy enactment in schools. In Section II, authors consider the disparity between intent and implementation of equity-focused policies in education. Also, authors include a focus on cross-system challenges stemming from incongruent provisions within various enacted policies. Examples of system intersection as well as intersectional social identity consideration include homelessness policies enacted in schools, the intersection of foster care and education policies and approaches within research, and immigration policies as experienced within education contexts. In Section III, authors provide exemplars of research that center the voices and perspectives of participants and consider both macro and micro contexts. Authors consider youth perspectives of the juvenile justice system during community reentry, Black male teachers' views and experiences, and community voice and collaboration in research design in Indigenous communities.

Our intention with this book is that readers from the policy, practice, and research arenas reflect on their own power, privilege, and positionality and consider the impact of the multiple identities that individuals adopt/ are assigned; move beyond discrete subgroup labels; and fully consider the interaction of such markers in the hegemonic, structural, and interpersonal domains that impact how education policy and research are developed, enacted, and experienced. We hope that readers have gained from the book an understanding of IBA as a tool to use to more authentically engage with intersectionality and to recognize the potential of this humanizing approach to dismantle power structures.

REFERENCES

Annamma, S., Connor, D., & Ferri, B. (2013). *DisCrit: Disability studies and critical race theory in education.* Teachers College Press.

Collins, P. H. (2015). Intersectionality's definitional dilemmas. *Annual Review of Sociology, 41,* 1–20.

Collins, P. H., & Bilge, S. (2016) *Intersectionality.* Polity Press.

Crenshaw, K. (1991). Mapping the margins: Intersectionality, identity politics, and violence against women of color. *Stanford Law Review, 43*(6), 1241–1299.

Hancock, A. (2007). Intersectionality as a normative and empirical paradigm. *Politics & Gender, 3*(2), 248–254. https://doi.org/10.1017/S1743923X07000062

Hankivsky, O., & Cormier, R. (2011). Intersectionality and public policy: Some lessons from existing models. *Political Research Quarterly, 64,* 217–229.

Hankivsky, O., Grace, D., Hunting, G., Giesbrecht, M., Fridkin, A., Rudrum, S., Ferlatte, O., & Clark, N. (2014). An intersectionality-based policy analysis framework: Critical reflections on methodology for advancing equity. *International Journal for Equity in Health, 13,* 119–135.

About the Contributors

Wendy Cavendish is a professor in the Department of Teaching and Learning at the University of Miami. Dr. Cavendish's interdisciplinary research focuses on identifying the practices and processes in schools and other social institutions (e.g., criminal justice system) that facilitate and support successful transition of youth both into and out of special education in ways that lead to positive outcomes. Her scholarly works converge at two interrelated lines of research: (a) the transition process for graduation and postschool preparation, and (b) the transition process for successful school and community reentry for juvenile justice-involved youth

Jennifer F. Samson is associate professor at Hunter College, City University of New York, and faculty associate at Roosevelt House Public Policy Institute. As a bilingual school psychologist and teacher educator, her equity-focused scholarship examines how best to prepare teachers to meet the needs of diverse learners. Dr. Samson studies the social, political, and systemic structures that impact learning and successful outcomes for culturally, linguistically, and ability-diverse students. Her research, practice, and policy-based work has been published and presented nationally and internationally.

Aydin Bal is a professor of education at the University of Wisconsin–Madison. His research focuses on the interplay among culture, learning, and mental health across local and global education systems. Dr. Bal examines the social justice issues in education, family–school–community–university collaboration, and systemic transformation. He has developed a Culturally Responsive Positive Behavioral Interventions and Supports framework and the Learning Lab methodology. In Learning Labs, local stakeholders (students, families, educators, policymakers, and community representatives), especially those from historically marginalized communities, collectively design and implement culturally responsive behavioral support systems. As a practitioner and researcher, Dr. Bal has worked with youth from minoritized communities experiencing academic and behavioral problems in schools, hospitals, and prisons from the United States, Turkey, South Sudan, Syria, the Russian Federation, Anishinaabe Nation, and Malawi.

Aaron Bird Bear (Mandan, Hidatsa, and Diné; enrolled Three Affiliated Tribes of Fort Berthold Indian Reservation) was appointed as the inaugural tribal relations director at the University of Wisconsin–Madison in 2019. Bird Bear joined UW–Madison in 2000 to support the retention and graduation of all American Indian, Alaska Native, and Native Hawaiian students at the university. In 2009, Bird Bear began supporting historically underrepresented precollege, undergraduate, and graduate/professional students in the UW–Madison School of Education as the assistant dean of student diversity programs. While in the School of Education, Bird Bear forwarded the school's efforts to fulfill the state statutes that mandate the instruction of the histories, cultures, and tribal sovereignty of the 11 First Nations of Wisconsin through the creation of the educator resource wisconsinfirstnations.org. Bird Bear is an alumnus of the Educational Leadership and Policy Analysis MS program at UW–Madison.

Patrice E. Fenton, PhD, is the founder and chief thought partner at the Fenton Collective, where her identity-responsive research drives her work as an equity-centered change strategist. With a passion for teacher development and recruitment, leadership development, and centering wellness in the workplace, Dr. Fenton has expertise in evaluating impact for Black and Brown communities. She has served as the director of leader support and development at EdLoC, a nonprofit professional network organization comprised of 350+ leaders of color across 30+ states. She is also the former associate director of NYC Men Teach at the City University of New York, a cross-agency initiative that exceeded the city's goal of recruiting 1,000 men of color to the public school teacher pipeline within 3 years. Dr. Fenton is an adjunct assistant professor at Hunter College and serves as a board member of South Bronx Community Charter High School, the Latinx Education Collaborative, and Disruptive Partners. She is also a proud Brooklyn, NY, native and mom to son, Jair Asad, and daughter, Haile Masani.

Osamudia James is a professor of law and Dean's Distinguished Scholar at the University of Miami Law School, where she writes and teaches in education law, race and the law, administrative law, and torts. She also serves as the associate dean for diversity, equity, and community at the School of Law, and the associate provost for diversity, equity, and inclusion at the university. Her scholarship and media commentary explore the interaction of law and identity in the context of public education, and her work has been published in the law reviews of New York University, the University of Iowa, and the University of Michigan, as well as in the pages of the *New York Times* and the *Washington Post*. She was a co-recipient of the 2014 Derrick A. Bell, Jr., Award, a national award presented to a junior faculty member who makes an extraordinary contribution to legal education, the legal system, or social justice through activism, mentoring, teaching, and scholarship; was awarded the Hausler Golden Apple Teaching Award in 2017; and is a 2020 University of Miami Public Voices Fellow. She holds a JD from Georgetown University Law Center and an LLM from the University of Wisconsin, where she was a William H. Hastie Fellow.

Kristin W. Kibler, PhD, is a former high school teacher and literacy coach with over a decade of experience in urban public schools. She is currently working as a lecturer in the Department of Teaching and Learning at the University of Miami. Her research interests center around improving educational outcomes and advancing equity for students from groups that have historically been minoritized and marginalized in the United States. To this end, she is interested in the promise of multicultural education and its social justice tenets, disability studies in education, critical literacy, cultural sustaining pedagogy, bilingual education, and education policy.

Dosun Ko is an assistant professor at Wichita State University. His research interests include racial disproportionality in behavioral outcomes (e.g., emotional behavioral disorder identification, school discipline); culturally responsive, inclusive education; and community-based design research grounded in cultural-historical activity theory.

Amie L. Nielsen is an associate professor in the Department of Sociology at the University of Miami. Her research interests and publications largely deal with the relationships between race, ethnicity, immigration, and crime and deviance, broadly defined, at both the individual and community levels. In addition, her recent work explores the roles of prejudice and racism for punitive attitudes among non-Latinx Whites.

Linda Orie is a graduate student in the Department of Curriculum and Instruction and a project assistant for the Department of Rehabilitation Psychology and Special Education at the University of Wisconsin–Madison. As part of the CRPBIS team, Linda serves as the main contact between study participants and the research team, helps design research materials and methods, and uses her experience as a former middle school science teacher to inform her contribution to the team's work. An enrolled member of the Oneida Nation of Wisconsin, Linda taught on a reservation in rural Northern Wisconsin from 2006 to 2012 and is interested in culturally responsive curriculum and pedagogy, systemic change, increasing the number of diverse teachers and educational leaders, and increasing equity in all forms in education. Linda earned bachelor's degrees from the University of Wisconsin–Oshkosh (BS elementary education '06) and Stanford University (BA psychology '03) and is currently completing her MS in curriculum and instruction at UW–Madison. She will continue on to the doctoral program and continue to work with the CRPBIS team during the implementation and sustainability phases of the Indigenous Learning Lab Project.

Leigh Patel is an educator, researcher, and writer. Her transdisciplinary research focuses on the ways that schooling acts as one of the most efficient delivery systems in society, as well as the potential for liberation through education. She is author of many publications, and her fifth book, *There Is No Study Without Struggle: Higher Education in a Settler Colony*, will be published by Beacon Press in 2021.

Deborah Perez is a doctoral candidate at the University of Miami in the Teaching and Learning Department. With a focus in special education, her research interests include using a community-based participatory action approach to further gain knowledge regarding systems change theory, interventions, policy advocacy, and critical social change, to improve the health and quality of life for all communities. Having experienced childhood poverty and traumas herself, Deborah is primarily dedicated to providing access and care to marginalized youth using an Emic perspective in pursuit of advancing educational research.

Kele Stewart is a professor and associate dean for experiential learning at the University of Miami School of Law. Her teaching, scholarship, and policy work focus on improving outcomes for children and families from under-resourced communities. Professor Stewart teaches family law and codirects the Children & Youth Law Clinic, where she supervises law students in civil and administrative cases on behalf of children and young adults in the foster care system. Her research addresses child welfare policy and its intersection with other systems that impact youth. She cofounded the University of Miami site of First Star Academy, an interdisciplinary practice and research initiative to provide holistic college readiness and social–emotional support to high school students in foster care. In 2011, Professor Stewart was awarded a J. William Fulbright Scholar grant to study child protection in her homeland of Trinidad and Tobago. Professor Stewart earned a BS in human development and family studies from Cornell University and a JD from New York University Law School.

Index

The letter *f* or *t* after a page number indicates a figure or table, respectively.

NAMES

SUBJECTS